TRUE OR FALSE?

This piece of gum could land someone in jail!

TRUE!

This gum was found at a crime scene. There were tooth marks on it. Investigators realized that this gum could be a clue. Maybe the gum chewer was the criminal!

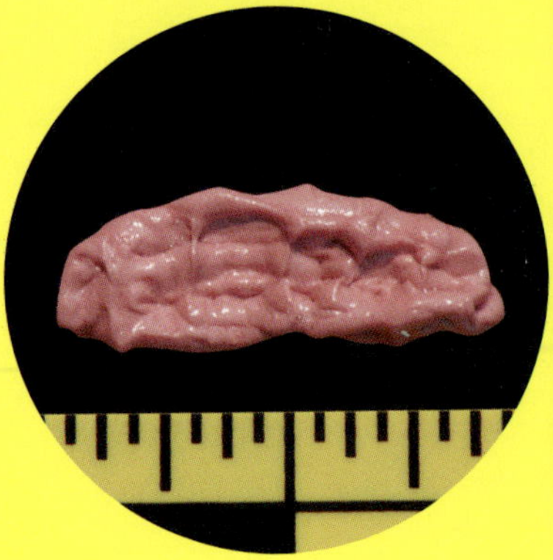

Investigators used the gum to make a mold that showed what the gum chewer's teeth looked like.

Then they compared this mold to a suspect's teeth. Faced with this mouthful of evidence, the suspect pled guilty!

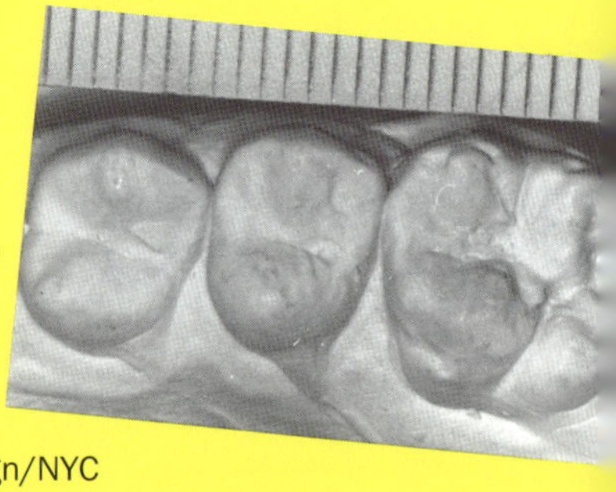

Book design Red Herring Design/NYC

Library of Congress Cataloging-in-Publication Data
Winchester, Elizabeth.
The right bite : dentists as detectives / by Elizabeth Siris Winchester.
p. cm. — (24/7: science behind the scenes)
Includes bibliographical references and index.
ISBN-13: 978-0-531-12062-0 (lib. bdg.) 978-0-531-18734-0 (pbk.)
ISBN-10: 0-531-12062-7 (lib. bdg.) 0-531-18734-9 (pbk.)
1. Dental jurisprudence—Juvenile literature. I. Title.
RA1062.W56 2007
614'.18–dc22 2006005874

1 2 3 4 5 6 7 8 9 10 R 16 15 14 13 12 11 10 09 08 07

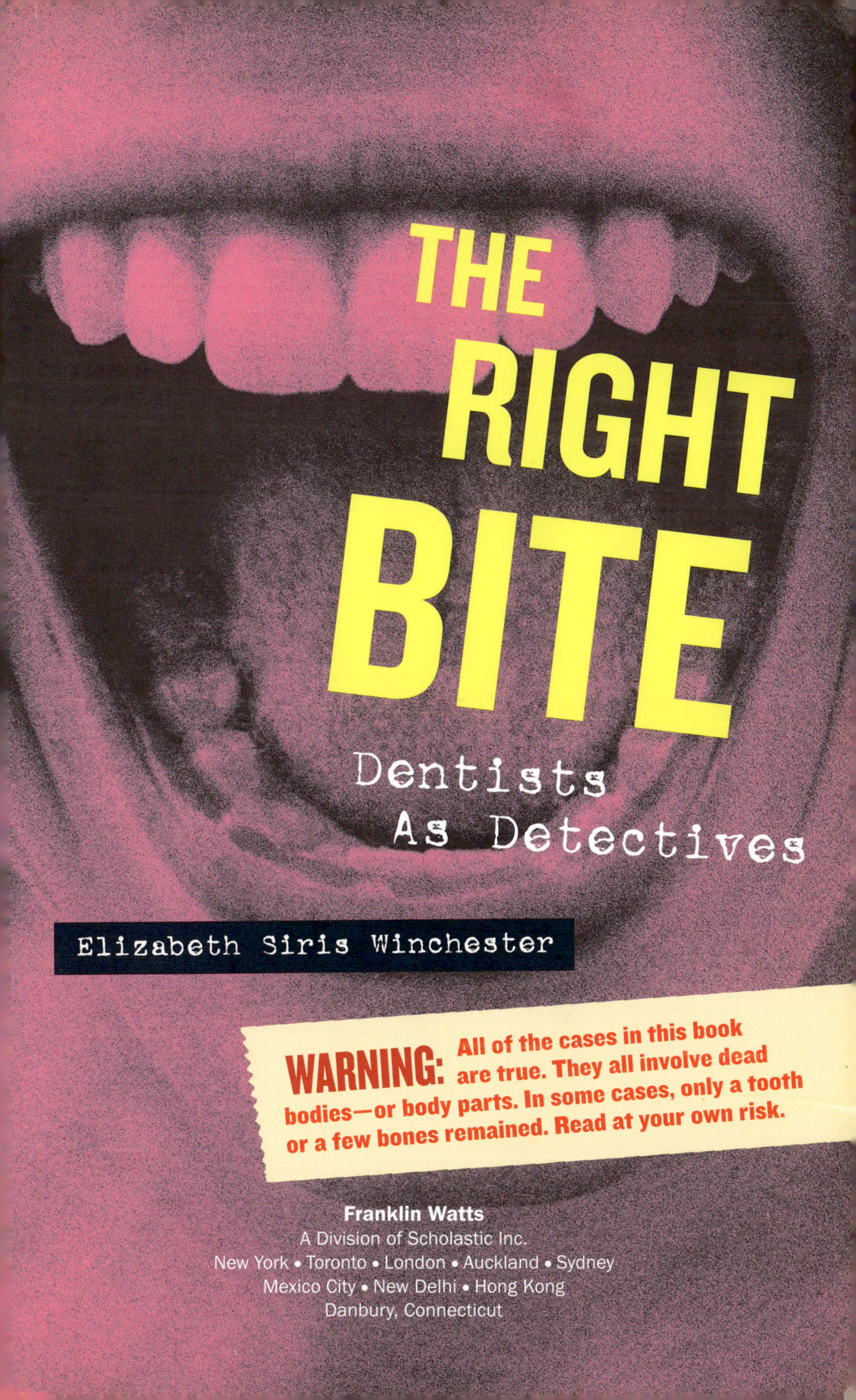

THE RIGHT BITE

Dentists As Detectives

Elizabeth Siris Winchester

WARNING: All of the cases in this book are true. They all involve dead bodies—or body parts. In some cases, only a tooth or a few bones remained. Read at your own risk.

Franklin Watts
A Division of Scholastic Inc.
New York • Toronto • London • Auckland • Sydney
Mexico City • New Delhi • Hong Kong
Danbury, Connecticut

CONTENTS

FORENSIC 411

Get the 411. Here's a mouthful of information about forensic dentists.

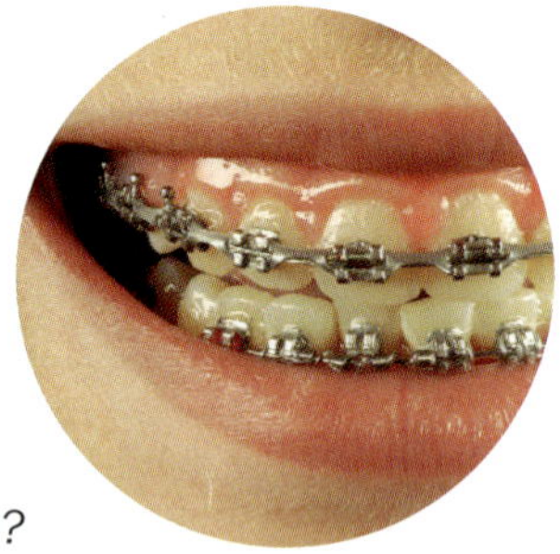

Troops search for a missing person near Moose Lake, MN.

TRUE-LIFE CASE FILES!

These cases are 100% real. Find out how forensic dentists solved some pretty intense mysteries.

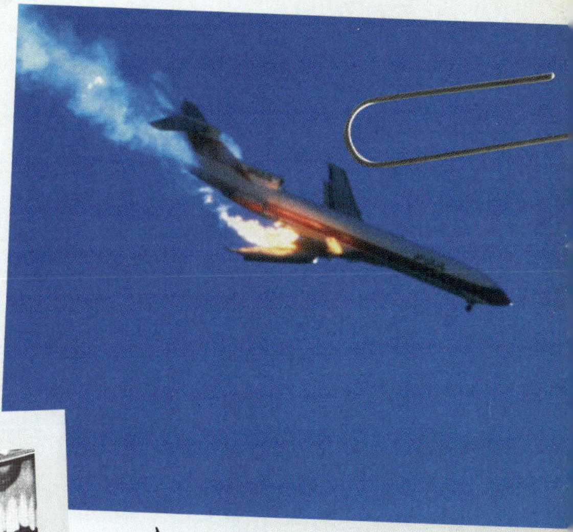

A plane crashes in San Diego, CA.

A forensic dentist speaks at a murder trial in Miami, FL.

FORENSIC DOWNLOAD

Here's even more amazing stuff about forensic dentistry for you to chew on.

YELLOW PAGES

FORENSIC 411

Forensic dentists work on real crimes and disasters. They use teeth to identify people. They examine the mouths of dead bodies to figure out who died. Sometimes, they help find criminals by their bitemarks.

IN THIS SECTION:

- how forensics dentists REALLY TALK;
- GROSS STUFF dentists look for in victims' mouths;
- who else is working at the CRIME SCENES.

Tooth Talk

Forensic dentists have their own way of talking. Find out what their vocabulary means.

"Get me an expert in **odontology** now! We need to try to figure out who this victim was by his teeth!"

odontology
(OH-don-TOL-oh-gee)
dentistry. The study of everything about teeth.

"Odonto" has to do with teeth. "Ology" means "the study of."

"Today, we've got a tough job. We must **identify** this body that was found in a fire."

identify
(eye-DEN-tuh-fye)
to find out who someone is

"Could someone please take notes? I am going to start examining the teeth of this **corpse**."

corpse
(korps)
a dead body

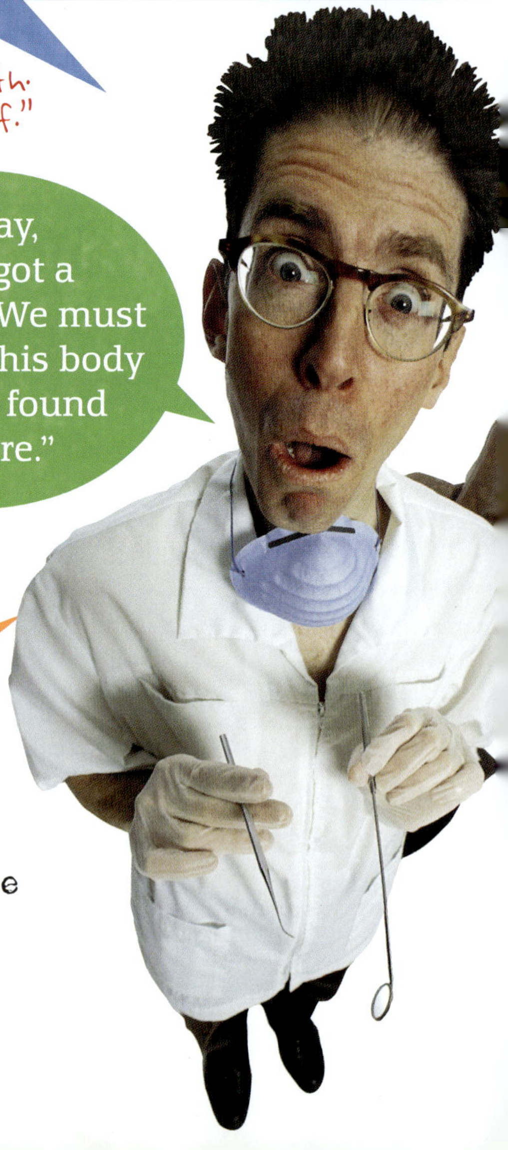

"Shine more light in the back of the corpse's mouth. I'm trying to do a **postmortem** exam here, and I need to see all his teeth."

postmortem
(pohst-MORE-tem)
after death. During a postmortem exam, the dentist makes notes about what a victim's teeth look like.

"Post" means "after."
"Mortem" means "death."

"This corpse is definitely not Mr. Smith. Mr. Smith's **antemortem** dental records show he was missing his front teeth!"

antemortem
(an-tee–MORE-tehm)
before death. Your antemortem dental records are all the x-rays and records from your visits to the dentist.

"Ante" means "before."

Say What?

Here's some other lingo forensic dentists might use on the job.

dupe
(doop) a copy. It's short for the word *duplicate*.
*"Make a **dupe** of the suspect's mouth so we can compare it to this bitemark."*

ID
(eye-DEE) to find out who a person is. It's short for the word *identify*.
*"We've got to **ID** the victims of this plane crash."*

reefer
(REE-fur) a huge, refrigerated trailer. It's short for the word *refrigerator*.
*"Let's move the victims' bodies to a **reefer** until we can examine them."*

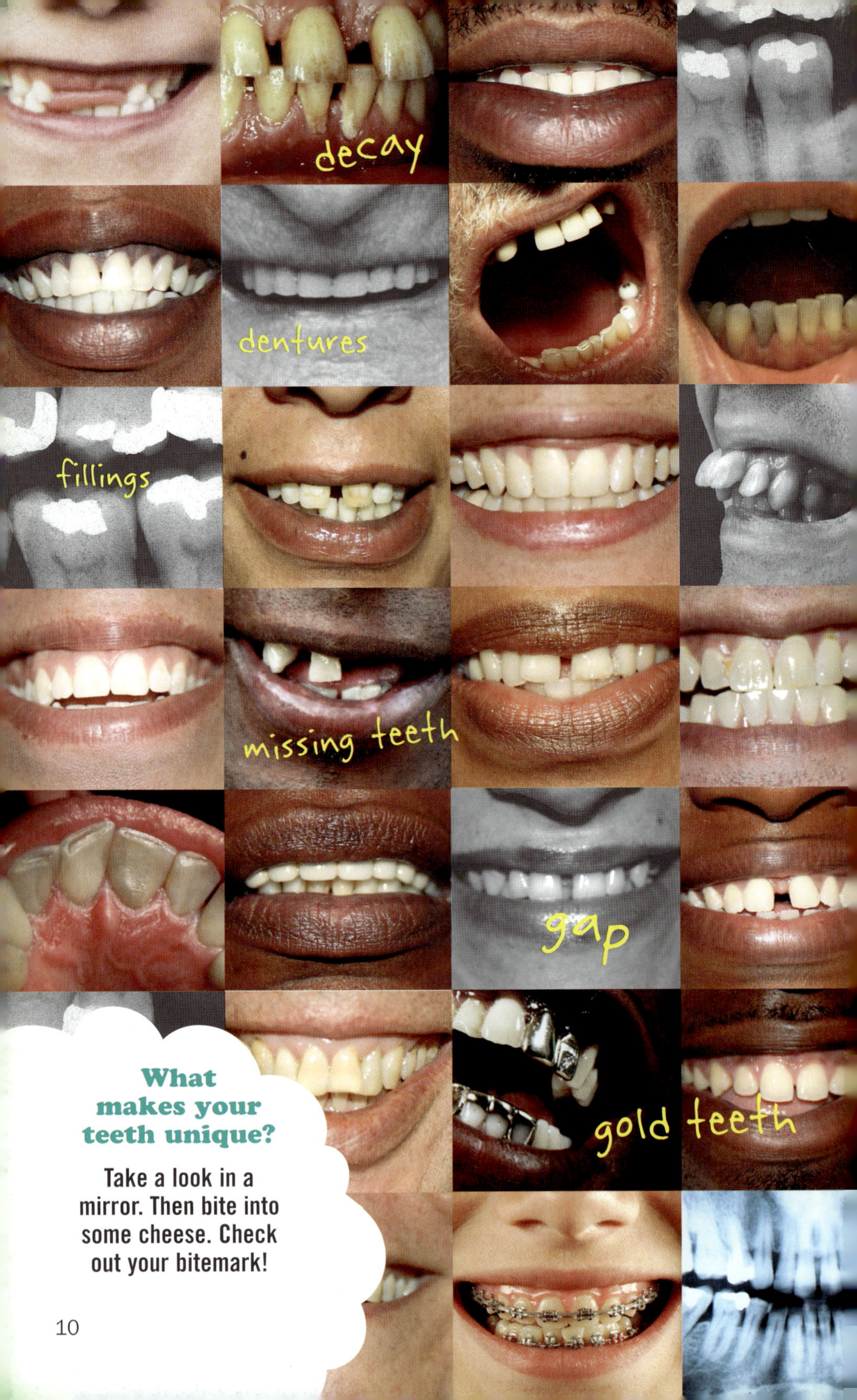

What makes your teeth unique?

Take a look in a mirror. Then bite into some cheese. Check out your bitemark!

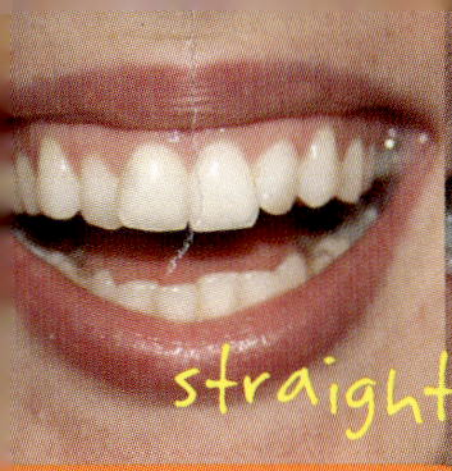

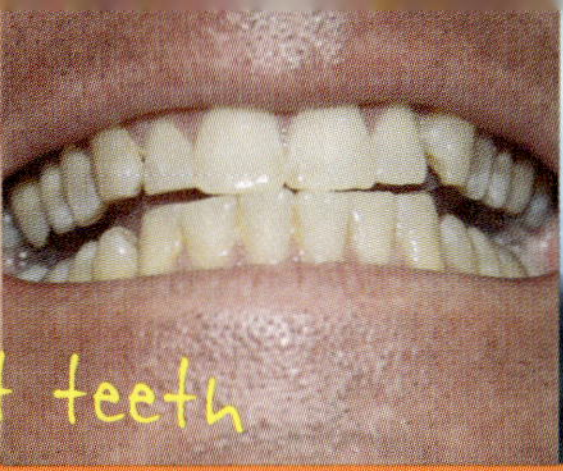

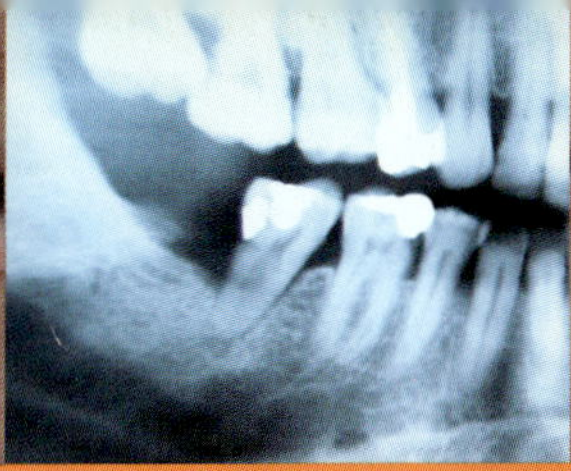

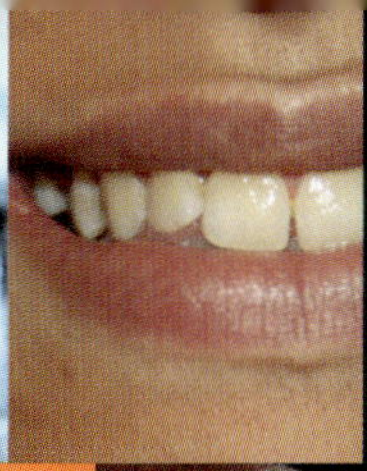

Your Teeth Say A Lot!

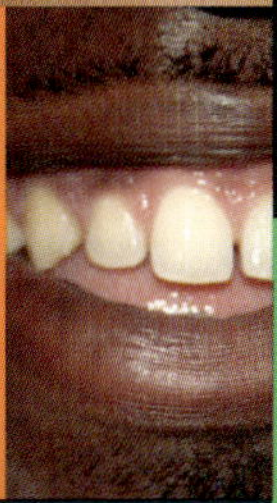

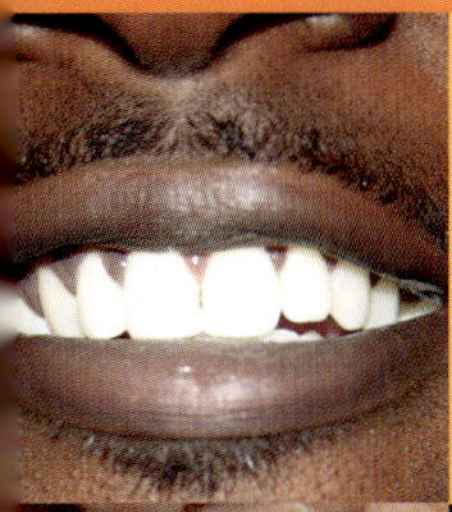

Chipped. Broken. Twisted. Turned! Everyone's teeth are different.

In fact, teeth are sort of like fingerprints. That's why they're such a good way of identifying people.

Say some **forensic dentists** need to identify a **victim** of a disaster. First, they take a close look at the victim's teeth to see what makes them unique. They make notes about what they find.

Next, say the dentists have some idea of who the victim might be. They'll track down the victim's old **dental records**. They'll study them carefully.

Then they compare all the evidence. Is there a match?

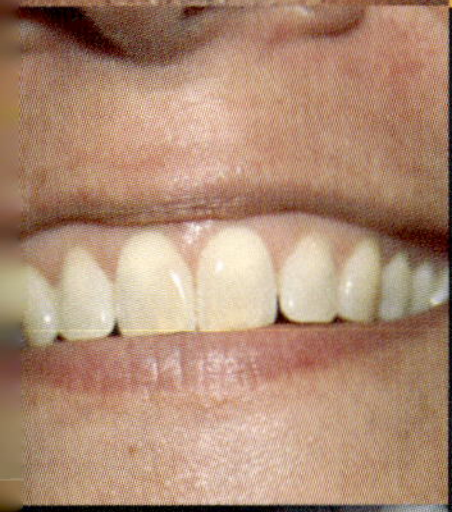

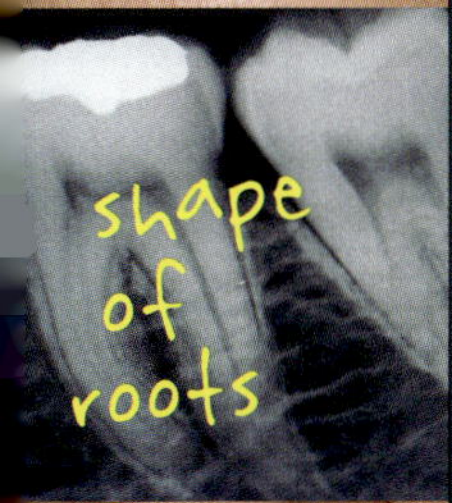

What makes teeth unique? Here's a list of some of the details that dentists look for.

- Do the teeth have **fillings**?
- Are they straight—or turned?
- Do any teeth have **crowns**—covers for damaged teeth?
- Are any teeth **impacted**—unable to grow out?
- Have any teeth been replaced by a **bridge**, or false tooth?
- Are any teeth missing or broken?
- How much space is between the teeth?
- Are the teeth discolored?

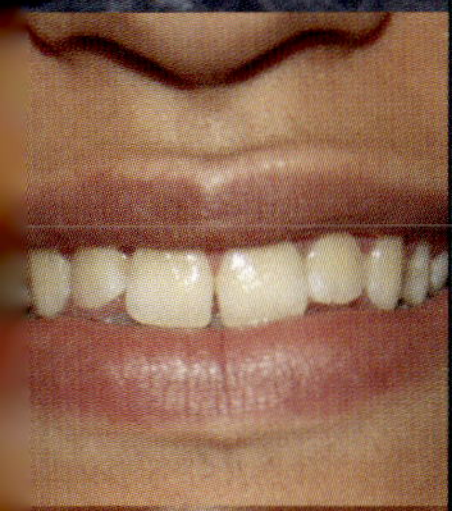

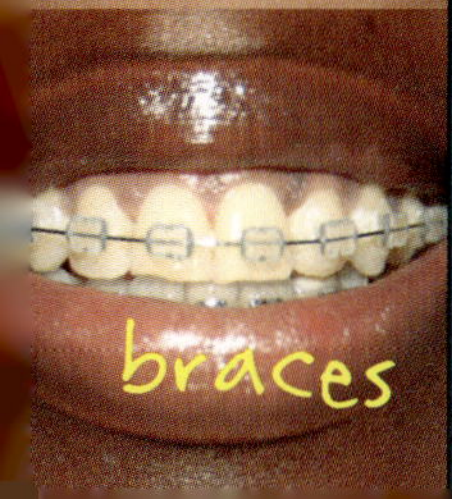

The Forensic Team

When there's a big case, forensic dentists work with other experts. Here's a look at some of them.

MEDICAL EXAMINERS

They're medical doctors who investigate suspicious deaths. They try to find out when and how someone died. They often direct other members of the team.

FORENSIC DNA SPECIALISTS

They collect DNA from blood or body fluids left at the scene. Then they use this evidence to identify victims and suspects.

FORENSIC ANTHROPOLOGISTS

They're called in to identify mysterious bones!

FORENSIC TOXICOLOGISTS

They're called in to test victims for drugs, alcohol, and/or poison.

FINGERPRINT EXAMINERS

They find, photograph, and collect fingerprints at the scene. Then, they compare them to prints they have on record.

FORENSIC DENTISTS

They identify victims and criminals by their teeth or bitemarks.

CRIMINALISTS

They sketch or photograph the scene. They also look for and collect evidence—such as blood, hair, paint, glass, fibers, weapons, and tire marks.

TRUE-LIFE CASE FILES!

24 hours a day, 7 days a week, 365 days a year, forensic dentists are solving mysteries.

IN THIS SECTION:

- how a dentist tried to solve a MYSTERY with just one tooth;
- how a team identified victims of a double PLANE CRASH;
- how investigators used a BITEMARK to track a killer.

24/7 Science Behind the Scenes

Here's how forensic dentists get the job done.

What does it take to solve a crime? Good forensic dentists don't just make guesses. They're scientists. They follow a scientific, step-by-step process.

As you read the case studies, you can follow along with them. Keep an eye out for the icons below. They'll clue you in to each step along the way.

At the beginning of each case, the forensic dentists identify ***one or two main questions*** they need to answer.

Their next step is to ***gather and analyze evidence***. Forensic dentists collect as much information as they can. They study it to figure out what it means.

Along the way, the forensic dentists come up with theories to explain what happened. They test these theories against the evidence. ***Does the evidence back up the theory?*** If so, they've reached a conclusion.

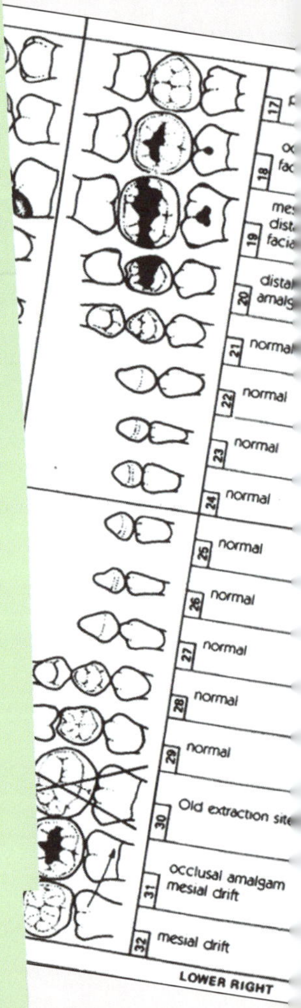

TRUE-LIFE CASE #1

Moose Lake, Minnesota
May 26, 1999
11:38 P.M.

Murder in Minnesota

**A young woman disappears.
Can one little tooth help scientists
solve the mystery?**

Missing Without a Trace

Katie Poirier vanishes with just a fuzzy videotape left behind.

Katie Poirier was 19 when she disappeared.

Although the security camera did not catch a picture of the kidnapper's face, it did get a picture of his shirt. He was wearing a Yankee's T-shirt.

Katie Poirier often worked nights at DJ's convenience mart about 45 miles (72 kilometers) from Duluth, Minnesota.

At 19, she was living at home with her parents. She had graduated from high school the year before. On May 26, 1999, Poirier showed up for the late shift—and never returned home.

At first, police didn't have much to go on. They pieced together Poirier's final moments at work from a fuzzy security video. At 11:38, Poirier had been alone in the store. A man walked in, grabbed her by the neck, and forced her outside. The video cameras didn't record the man's face. They did catch his shirt. It was a New York Yankees T-shirt with the number 23 on it. Police found just one possible witness. A woman who worked nearby saw a drunken man at the store that night. The man drove a black Ford pickup truck. She remembered a portion of the license plate. It read 557__ Y.

Was the evidence enough to lead police to the criminal?

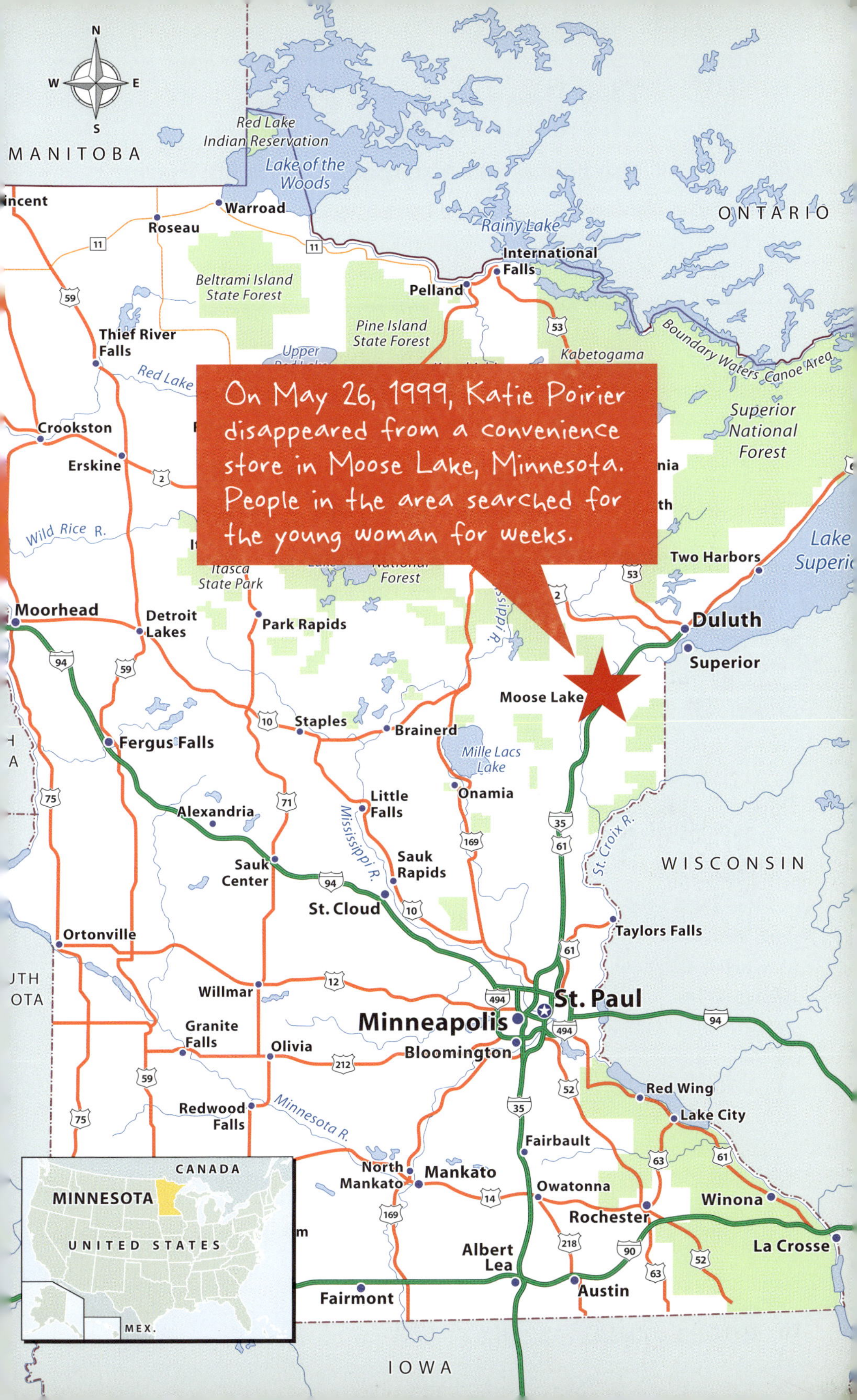
On May 26, 1999, Katie Poirier disappeared from a convenience store in Moose Lake, Minnesota. People in the area searched for the young woman for weeks.
N
S
E
W
MANITOBA
ONTARIO
WISCONSIN
IOWA
Red Lake Indian Reservation
Lake of the Woods
Rainy Lake
Warroad
Roseau
International Falls
Pelland
Beltrami Island State Forest
Pine Island State Forest
Kabetogama
Boundary Waters Canoe Area
Superior National Forest
Thief River Falls
Red Lake
Crookston
Erskine
Wild Rice R.
Itasca State Park
Forest
Two Harbors
Lake Superior
Moorhead
Detroit Lakes
Park Rapids
Duluth
Superior
Moose Lake
Staples
Brainerd
Fergus Falls
Mille Lacs Lake
Onamia
Little Falls
Alexandria
Mississippi R.
Sauk Centre
Sauk Rapids
St. Cloud
St. Croix R.
Taylors Falls
Ortonville
Willmar
St. Paul
Minneapolis
Granite Falls
Olivia
Bloomington
Redwood Falls
Minnesota R.
Red Wing
Lake City
Fairbault
North Mankato
Mankato
Owatonna
Winona
Rochester
La Crosse
Albert Lea
Austin
Fairmont
CANADA
MINNESOTA
UNITED STATES
MEX.

The Search for a Killer

The police find a suspect. Did he kill Poirier?

For three weeks, police searched for Katie Poirier. A home video of her, smiling in her kitchen, played again and again. Local and national TV stations followed the case. Hundreds of volunteers joined the hunt.

Police searched for the kidnapper as well. They drew a sketch of the suspect. Finally, a tip from a coworker led police to Donald Blom. Blom was 51. He owned a cabin near the store. He had a long criminal record. He sometimes wore a New York Yankees T-shirt. And he drove a black pickup truck. The license plate read 557 HDY.

The community was concerned about Katie Poirier. Volunteers took part in highly organized searches for her.

On June 18, the police went to search Blom's cabin. On his land, they found a fire pit. They went through the ashes in the pit. They made a horrible discovery. They found several pieces of bone—both human and animal.

But whose bones were they? A **forensic anthropologist** arrived at the scene to help. She studied the size and shape of the bones. Then she came up with a conclusion. The bones belonged to a small female between the

Fire pit, where a tooth and bone were found, is circled in red.

This photo was taken from the air. It shows Blom's trailer home near Moose Lake, MN. Investigators moved it off its foundation to search for signs of Poirier.

ages of 16 and 25. Katie was 19 when she was kidnapped.

Did that prove the bones were hers?

No. They could have belonged to any small missing female between 16 and 25.

The investigators needed another clue. They found it in the fire pit. Under the ashes lay a single lower **molar** (tooth #18). They also found a two-inch (five-cm) piece of jawbone to go with it.

It was time to bring in a forensic dentist.

To see where tooth #18 is, go to page 48.

The Minnesota National Guard joined the search for Poirier. Here, they're returning to their base on June 23, 1999. They've just searched the woods near Blom's trailer.

Forensic Dentist Called In

The tooth is handed over to Dr. Ann Norrlander. She starts her investigation.

Dr. Ann Norrlander joined the case. She's a forensic dentist.

Norrlander knew that she had to answer one main question. Did the tooth belong to Katie Poirier?

Norrlander had done more than 600 forensic exams. She knew that it might be possible to identify a victim from a single tooth. But the tooth has to be very unusual to be useful. She wished the police had found more teeth!

Dr. Ann Norrlander is a forensic dentist from Minneapolis, MN.

But Norrlander knew she'd have to work with what she had. She'd examine the tooth carefully. She'd look for any markings or fillings that made that tooth different from other teeth. Then, she'd examine Katie's antemortem dental records. She'd see if the tooth matched any on these records.

Soon, a **FBI** agent showed up at Norrlander's office. He had a small box. The tooth was inside.

Norrlander got to work. She examined the tooth.

She observed that it was missing the **enamel**. That's the hard stuff that covers a tooth. "Losing enamel is typical in a hot fire," Dr. Norrlander says. "But it made my task more difficult." It would be harder to tell if there had been marks on the tooth.

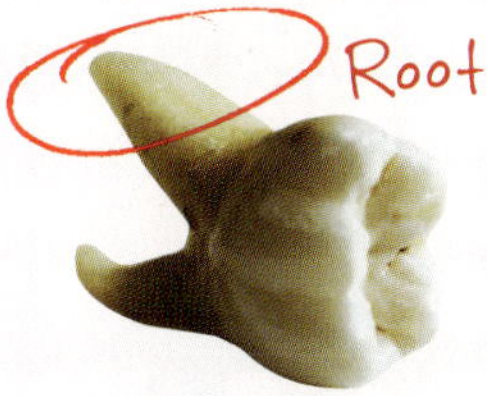

This is tooth #18. That's the kind of tooth that was found in Blom's fire pit.

Norrlander also examined the **roots** of the tooth. The roots attach a tooth to the jawbone. She observed that the roots of this tooth were oddly shaped. And the tooth actually had an extra root!

In fact, this tooth was so strange that Norrlander wasn't completely sure it had come from a human! Could it have come from an animal—like a deer? She took it to a veterinarian to find out.

The vet told her the tooth didn't come from a deer. This tooth definitely came from a human.

FBI agents collected ash from Donald Blom's fire pit. They stored it in this can. They then sent it to Norrlander's lab for her to examine.

EVIDENCE

Study That Tooth!

Okay, the tooth came from a human. What else could Dr. Norrlander learn about it?

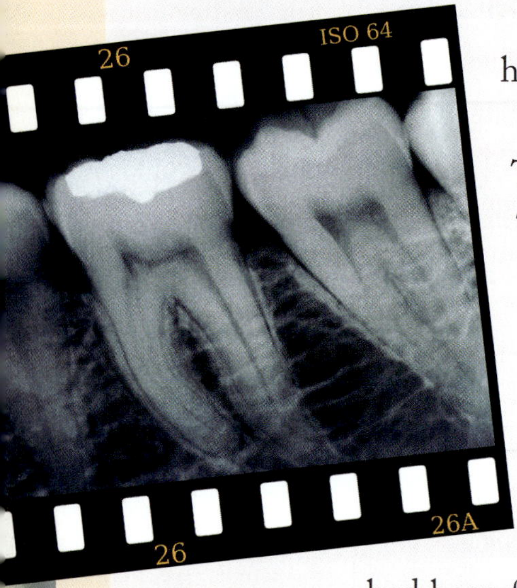

Norrlander now knew the tooth was human. But did it belong to Poirier?

Norrlander and her partner, Dr. Tom Rumreich, took a closer look. They examined the tooth under a **microscope**.

They also took **x-rays**. When they studied these x-rays, they saw that the tooth showed signs of dental work. The biting surface had markings on it where a cavity had been filled.

Forensic dentists like Dr. Norrlander often use victims' antemortem x-rays to help with identifications.

Norrlander looked again at the surface of the tooth. She found small amounts of a metallic material. Norrlander sent a sample to a lab. The lab found **traces** of a metal called zinc. They also found silver and other metals.

The evidence led to new questions. Did Poirier have a filling in tooth #18? If so, did it contain silver, zinc, and other metals?

A Call to Katie Poirier's Dentist

Dr. Norrlander and Dr. Rumreich requested Poirier's antemortem dental records. Would the records for her tooth #18 be similar to the tooth from the fire pit?

When the files arrived, the dentists had their answer. Yes, x-rays of Poirier's tooth #18 looked very much like the x-rays of the tooth from the fire pit. Also, she had had tooth #18 filled in 1991. And the **dentist** used a material with silver, zinc, and other metals to fill it.

The evidence was piling up. Norrlander was ready to say that the tooth possibly belonged to Poirier. But Norrlander needed to find more similarities to be sure.

Norrlander returned to the dental records. Poirier had been to the dentist just two weeks before she disappeared. Tooth #18 had been bothering her. The dentist replaced her filling.

The filling wasn't unusual. But another material the dentist used was. She used a new material called RelyX. It contains a rare metal called zirconium. So Norrlander sent the tooth to the lab to test it for zirconium.

The lab **experts** had big news for Norrlander. There was zirconium on the tooth.

Norrlander made her final conclusion. The tooth likely belonged to Katie Poirier.

Norrlander knew that Katie's dentist had used an unusual kind of material on Katie's teeth. It is called RelyX. It contains a rare metal called zirconium.

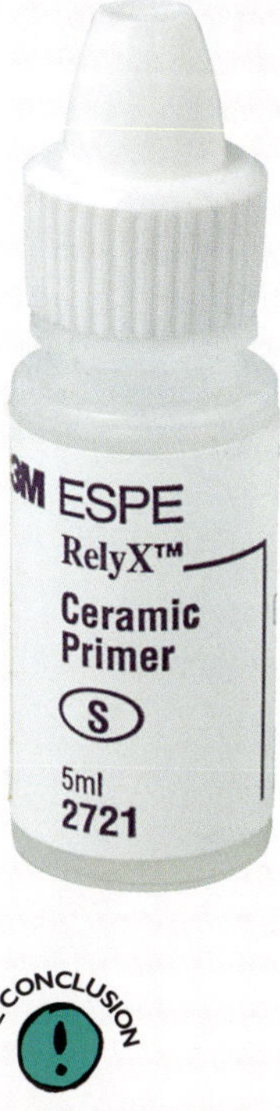

THE CONCLUSION

In Court

Was there enough evidence to convict Donald Blom?

Donald Blom went on trial in July 2000. He was charged with kidnapping and murdering Katie Poirier. The prosecution's case depended on Norrlander's evidence. She told the jury why she believed it was likely that the tooth was Poirier's.

In the trial, Blom's lawyers put their own forensic dentist on the witness stand. He disagreed with Norrlander's conclusion. The tooth, he claimed, could have possibly belonged to Katie Poirier. But he did not agree that it likely belonged to her.

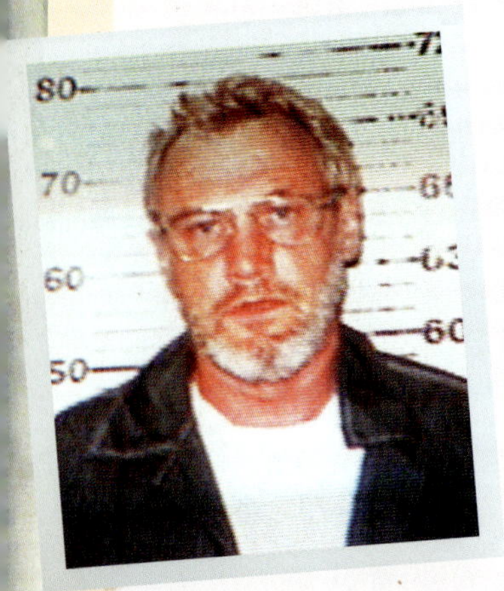

On August 16, 2000, a jury found Donald Bloom guilty of kidnapping and murder.

The jury, however, believed Norrlander. On August 16, they found Donald Blom guilty of kidnapping and murder. He was sent to jail for the rest of his life.

After the case, Dr. Norrlander talked about her work. "I feel strongly that the person I identified was Katie," she says. "But the trial never brings a person back. It's still a hard case for her family and for so many people in Minnesota." 24/7

In this case, forensic dentists used a single tooth to identify a person. In the next case, you'll find out how they identified victims of a big disaster.

TRUE-LIFE CASE #2

The Case of the Double Plane Crash

How would forensic dentists face the painful task of identifying more than 100 victims?

San Diego, California
September 26, 1978
9:01 A.M.

On the morning of September 25, 1978, two planes were preparing to land at the airport in San Diego, California. The planes crashed in mid air. Within about 15 seconds, both planes hit the ground.

One of the planes was a small Cessna. It fell to the ground near Lindbergh Field.

The other plane was a Boeing 727. That's a passenger plane. The remains of that plane landed in a San Diego neighborhood called North Park.

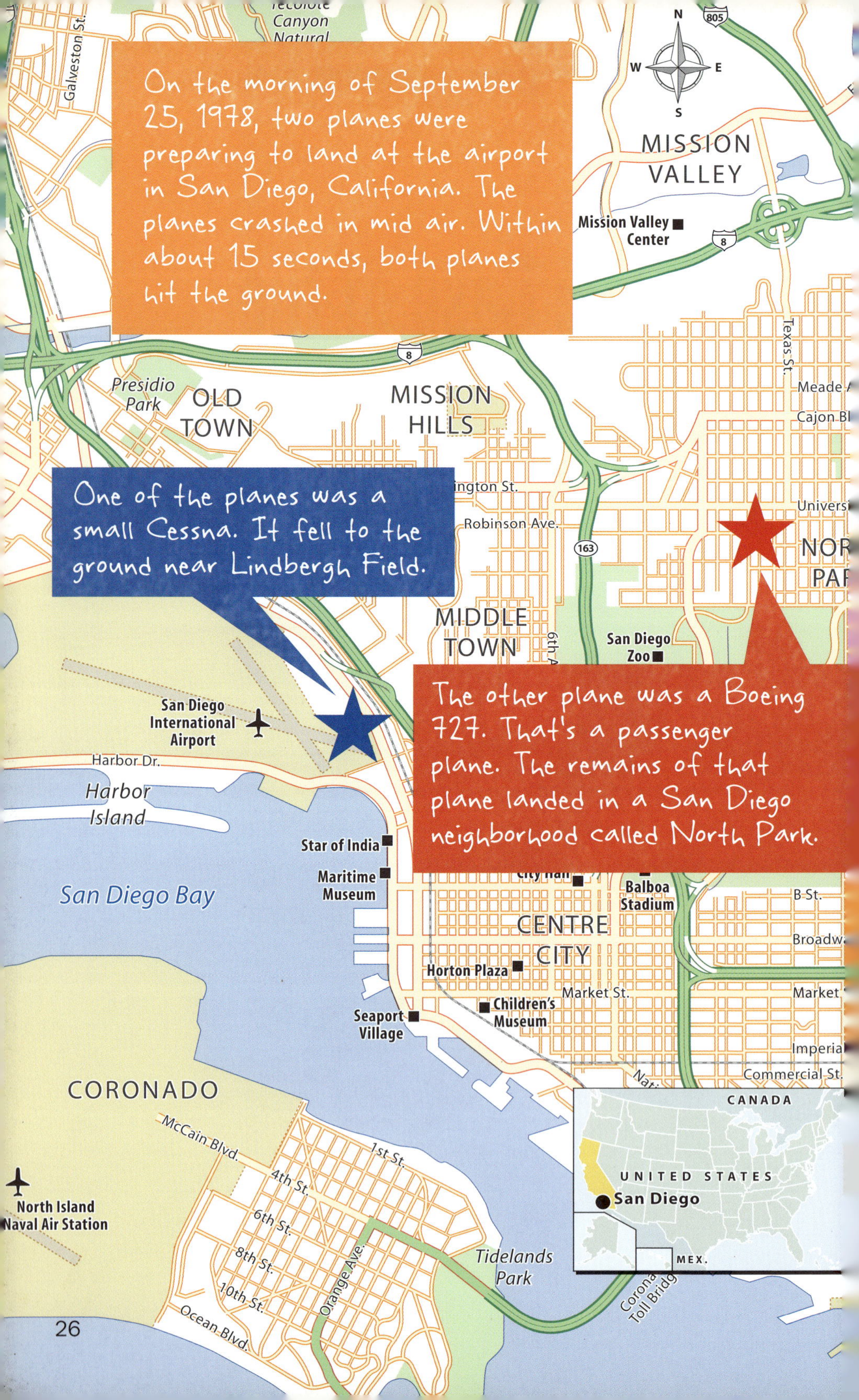

Plane Crash!

A terrible tragedy strikes in sunny southern California.

September 25, 1978, began clear and warm in San Diego. The sun shone through a blue sky. The temperature hovered around 80°F (27°C). It looked like the perfect day.

At 9 A.M., Pacific Southwest Airlines Flight 182 approached the airport. Its 135 passengers had a clear view of the city.

Then, at 2,600 feet (792 m), disaster struck. The jetliner crashed head-on into a small, single-engine Cessna. Flight 182 burst into flames. Both planes spun wildly toward the earth.

In about 15 seconds, both planes hit the ground. They crashed in crowded areas of the city. Flames leaped from the wreckage. A huge cloud of black and orange smoke rose to the sky.

A small, single-engine Cessna like this one flew into a Boeing 727 passenger plane.

San Diego police rushed to the scene. Everything was in chaos. "It was absolutely shocking to see the wreckage of the plane," police officer Bill Robinson told *San Diego Magazine*. "There were pieces of bodies all about, hanging from trees and telephone poles."

Below: The right wing of the Boeing 727 was on fire as the plane fell to the earth.
Right: The 727 landed in a crowded San Diego neighborhood. Twenty-two homes were destroyed. Seven people on the ground were killed.

Coroners investigate sudden or suspicious deaths.

Police knew right away there would be few survivors. They also knew that it would be very difficult to identify the dead. The San Diego County **coroner** needed to put together a team. And he needed to do it quickly. He picked up the phone and started to make calls.

An Impossible Task

Could Dr. Sperber and his team of forensic dentists help give names to the dead?

At 9:15 A.M., Dr. Skip Sperber got a call from the coroner. He was to report to the crash site immediately.

Investigators examine a jet engine at the accident site.

Sperber is a forensic dentist. He had plenty of experience identifying bodies. But when he got to the crash site, he was shocked.

It was the worst mid-air disaster in the United States to date. Everyone in the planes had died. In addition, seven people on the ground had been killed. In all, there were 144 victims around the crash site.

Sperber says he had never seen anything like it. Many of the bodies barely looked human. Some bodies had been torn to pieces. Many of the remains were badly burned.

THE QUESTION ?

Sperber had a tough job. How could he identify as many of the 144 victims as possible? The victims' families would want the remains of their loved ones. "People are given a name when they are born," Sperber says. "We try to give people a name when they die."

Sperber's Plan

Dr. Sperber put together three teams to help identify the victims.

Sperber knew he needed some help. He called **dentists** he knew. He also called **dental hygienists** and **dental assistants**.

Then he divided his group into three teams. Those teams were the antemortem team, the postmortem team, and the comparison team.

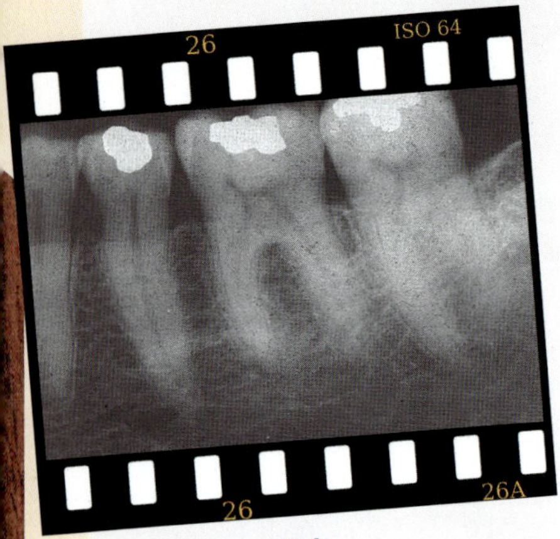

Forensic dentists examine victims' antemortem x-rays to look for unusual roots and other details that make someone's teeth unique. They also x-ray victims' teeth during postmortem exams.

The Before-Death Team

The antemortem team got to work right away. Sperber's partner, Dr. Robert Siegal, headed this team. He and his team worked at the coroner's office. They were in charge of finding dental records for the victims. They started by calling the families of the planes' passengers. The families put them in touch with the victims' dentists.

THE EVIDENCE

Siegal and his assistants studied the old dental records. They kept files for each victim. Under each name they listed anything unusual. They looked for fillings and crowns. They noted teeth with strange shapes or odd roots. Hopefully, these lists would help match victims to their remains.

The After-Death Team

Meanwhile, the postmortem team was studying the remains of the victims. Sperber led this group.

After the crash, rescue workers had worked around the clock to collect remains. They sorted body parts as best they could. Then they zipped the remains into body bags. The bags were placed in huge refrigerated trailers called reefers.

Members of the postmortem team examined the body bags, one by one. They worked in groups of three. That way, they could check one another's work.

First, they'd remove a bag from the reefer. They'd take it to an exam room in the coroner's office.

Then, they removed the jaws from the body. One examiner would describe the victim's mouth. Were there teeth missing? Which teeth had been filled? Which were shaped oddly? A second person looked on to make sure no details were missed. The third person took notes.

The teams also took x-rays of each pair of jaws. The x-rays would pick up more details.

Quickly, the records piled up inside the coroner's office.

The Comparison Team

The antemortem and postmortem teams worked in 12-hour shifts. As they collected information, they passed it on to the comparison team.

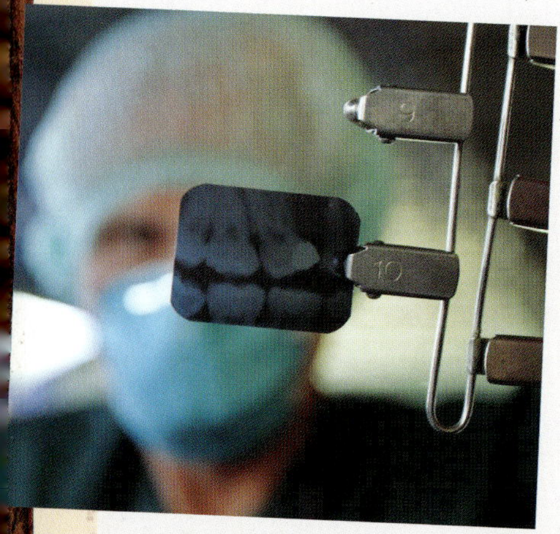

The comparison team spends countless hours reviewing dental records and the victims' teeth.

THE EVIDENCE

The comparison team had a huge job. It had nearly 150 sets of notes to match up with dental records.

But fortunately, they had a new tool. Dr. Sperber and Dr. Siegal had developed a computer program. It would compare antemortem and postmortem records. And it would identify possible matches.

It was the first time such a computer program had been used in a civilian disaster. "It sped up the whole identification process," Sperber said.

Identifications

Sperber and his team identified most of the victims.

THE CONCLUSION

The experts examined each of the 144 victims. Sperber and his team were able to identify all but four of the victims from the crash.

In another case, Skip Sperber shows how he identified a victim by her teeth.

As soon as the victims were identified, their remains were returned to their families. These families had experienced tremendous loss. But having their loved ones' remains often helped them cope. And Sperber was glad that he could use his skills to help. "I think it's my way of contributing to the community," he says. 24/7

ARE YOU SURE?

Some identifications are more definite than others.

At the end of a case, the lead forensic dentist looks at the victim's chart. She goes over the dental x-rays taken before and after the victim died. Then she makes one of the following conclusions.

positive ID: The antemortem and postmortem records are from the same person.

possible ID: The records are similar, but there isn't enough information to prove that they are from the same person.

insufficient evidence: There is not enough information to figure out who the person is.

exclusion: The antemortem and postmortem data are not from the same person.

Dr. Skip Sperber tells why teeth are often the only way to ID victims.

24/7: Is forensic dentistry often used to identify victims of plane crashes?

DR. SPERBER: Yes. Teeth are the hardest parts of the body. They do burn. But they don't burn as easily as other parts of the body. When a plane crashes and sets on fire, it usually doesn't reach a high enough temperature to severely burn teeth.

24/7: What is DNA? And isn't that a good way to identify people?

DR. SPERBER: DNA is the stuff in your cells that makes you different from everyone else. Testing victims' DNA can be a great way of identifying them.

24/7: Why didn't you use DNA to identify people after the plane crash?

DR. SPERBER: It wasn't available. This technology wasn't widely used until maybe 15 years ago.

24/7: So do people still use forensic dentistry to identify people? Or do they just use DNA?

DR. SPERBER: They still use forensic dentistry. Dental identifications are less costly and faster than DNA tests. Also, DNA evidence can be damaged if it's not stored carefully.

Forensic dentists don't just identify the dead. They also help police find criminals. Find out how in this next case.

TRUE-LIFE CASE #3

Tallahassee, Florida
January 15, 1978
12:00–2:00 A.M.

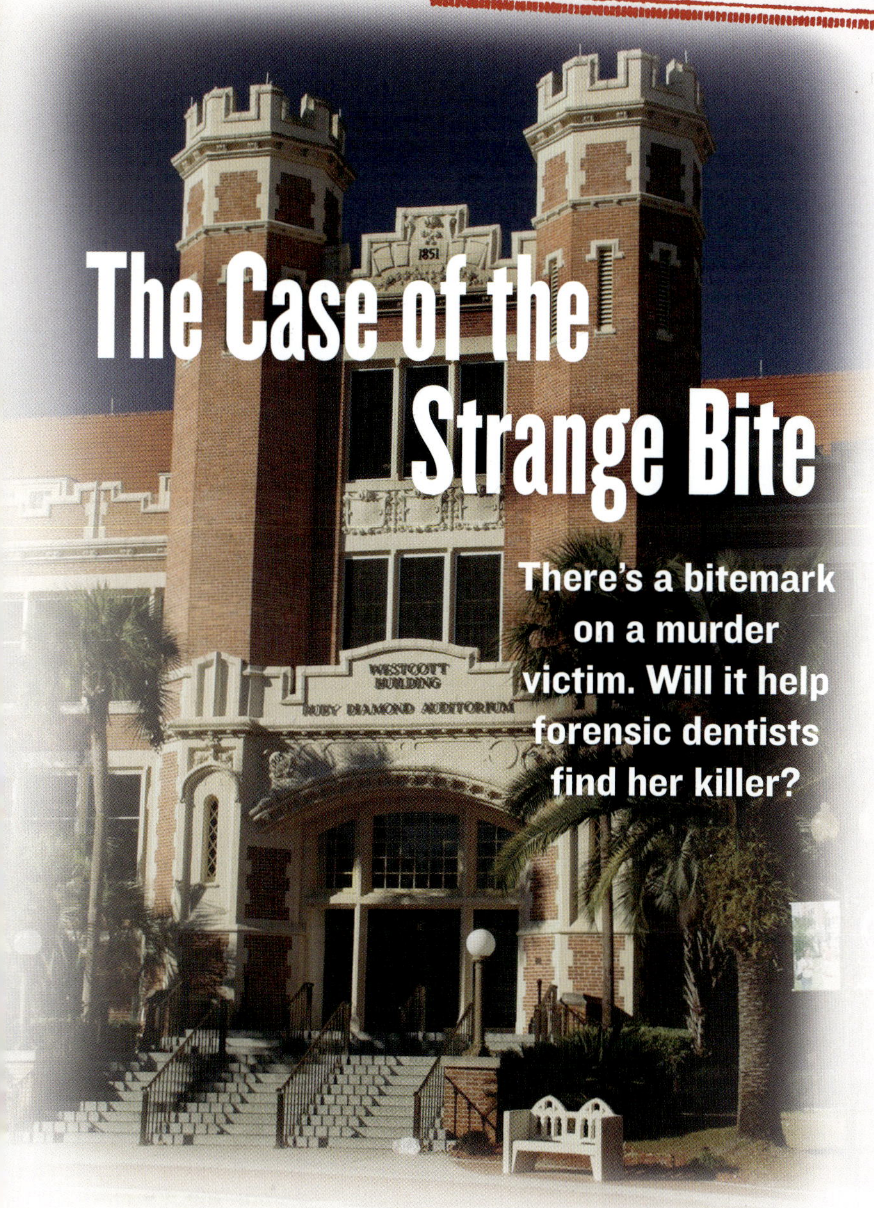

The Case of the Strange Bite

There's a bitemark on a murder victim. Will it help forensic dentists find her killer?

A Gruesome Crime

Two college students were killed. Two more were hurt. Were there any clues?

Lisa Levy, 20, was a student at Florida State University when she was killed.

It is probably the most famous **bitemark** case in history.

It all started on January 15, 1978. It was the middle of the night. A killer broke into a house in Tallahassee, Florida. Several female students from nearby Florida State University lived there. Two women, Lisa Levy and Margaret Bowman, were killed. Two other women who lived at the house were hurt.

The killer had been careful not to leave any clues. There were no fingerprints. He had carefully wiped them away.

But the killer did make one big mistake. He had bitten one of the murder victims, Lisa Levy. There was a bitemark on her. Could investigators find out who bit Lisa? If they could, they knew they'd have their killer.

Margaret Bowman, 21, was another victim. She was also a student at Florida State.

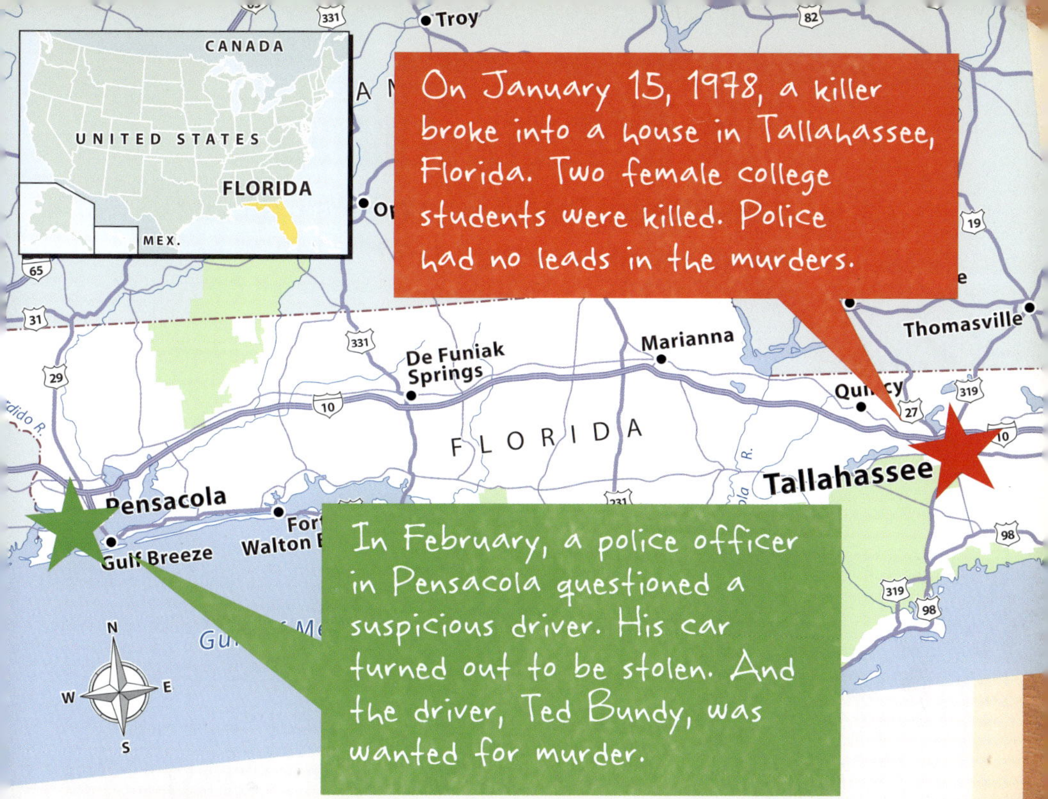

A Lucky Break

At first, there were no suspects in the case. Then a month after the murder, the police got a lucky break.

A man was picked up in nearby West Pensacola for driving a stolen car. He was identified as Ted Bundy. Bundy was a wanted man. He had been arrested in Colorado for the murder of a woman. But he had escaped from jail before his trial. Investigators thought he might have also killed women in the Pacific Northwest.

Was it possible that Bundy was also responsible for the murders of the college students?

The Bitemark Evidence

Dr. Richard Souviron, a forensic dentist, was called onto the case.

Now that the police had a suspect, they called Dr. Richard Souviron for help.

Souviron had been a forensic dentist in Florida for ten years.

The only evidence in the case was the bitemark on Lisa Levy. Could Souviron find out if Bundy had left that bitemark? To do that, Souviron would have to compare the bitemark to Bundy's actual teeth.

First, Souviron got to work on the bitemark. He asked the police for good photos of the bitemark—with a ruler next to it. That would show him the exact size of the bitemark.

Next, Souviron started to gather information about Bundy's teeth. He wanted to make an exact model of Bundy's mouth. To do that, Souviron would have to examine Bundy's mouth.

Souviron and the police had to ask for special permission from a judge to examine Bundy's mouth. They managed to

Ted Bundy was the main suspect in the case. Dr. Souviron knew that he'd have to examine Bundy's mouth to find out if it matched the bitemark.

get the permission. Now it was time for Bundy to open up and say, "Ahhh."

Making a Good Impression

That spring, Souviron met Bundy in a dental office in Tallahassee. The chief of police, eight police officers, two dentists, a doctor, and a lawyer were there.

Then the police officer told Bundy that Souviron was going to make a model of his teeth. Bundy started to sweat. "He was very scared," says Souviron.

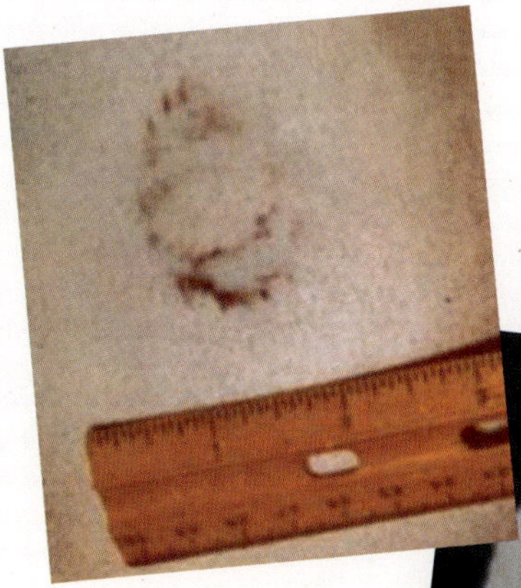

Left: The bitemark from Lisa Levy. The ruler shows the size of the mark. _Below:_ The model that Dr. Souviron made of Bundy's teeth. This model matched the bitemark.

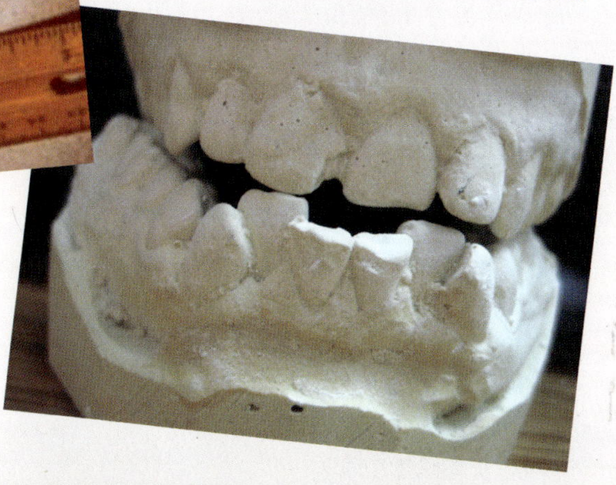

Souviron put his equipment on a metal tray. He asked the suspect, "Mr. Bundy, you're not going to bite me, are you?"

"No," Bundy said. "I'm a very non-violent person."

Souviron asked Bundy to open his mouth. The dentist made a model of Bundy's teeth.

Souviron also took photographs of Bundy's teeth. And he asked Bundy to bite into wax so he would have a record of how his teeth fit together.

Ted Bundy under arrest.

Souviron discovered that Bundy's teeth were very unusual. According to Souviron, he had "three chip marks on his upper front teeth." He also had a "crooked pattern in the lower teeth."

Souviron compared what he found to photographs of the bitemark. He realized he had a match. "The model and the

THE CONCLUSION !

picture of the bitemark fit together like a key in a lock," he says. He had found the killer.

On Trial

How would Dr. Souviron prove that Bundy was the biter?

Bundy's case went to trial in 1979. Dr. Souviron was under a lot of pressure. "There was no other physical evidence but the bitemark," he says. What's more, bitemark evidence had never been used at such a big trial.

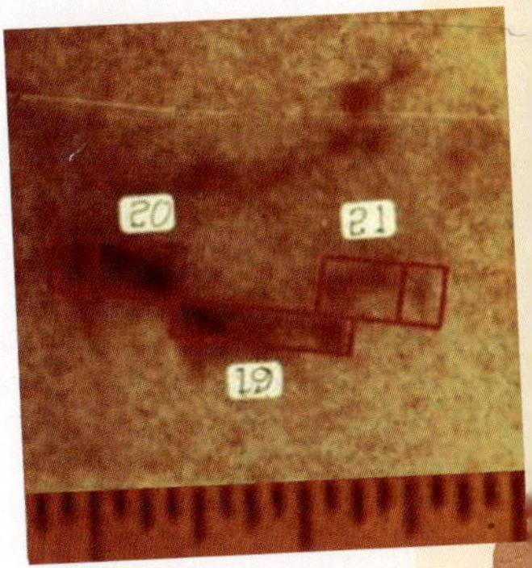

This diagram shows that Bundy's teeth matched the bitemark.

During the trial, Souviron explained how the bitemark matched Bundy's teeth. He showed a large photo of the bitemark. Then he placed a large picture of Bundy's teeth on top of the photo. He showed how Bundy's teeth fit exactly into the bitemark.

Bundy was found guilty of the murder of the college students. He was also found guilty of the murder of another young woman. He was sentenced to death and was executed ten years later.

Ted Bundy was arrested in Florida on February 15, 1978. He was found guilty of the murders of students Lisa Levy and Margaret Bowman on June 25, 1979.

Dr. Souviron was pleased that his work helped stop a dangerous killer from harming others. "It's extremely satisfying to play a small part in the criminal justice system," he says. "If I can contribute some information that helps justice get served, I'm glad to do my part." 24/7

Dr. Richard Souviron is a forensic dentist from Coral Gables, FL.

Dr. Richard Souviron
talks about bitemarks.

24/7: Was the Bundy case your first bitemark case?

DR. SOUVIRON: No. I had done a couple before. One involved a dog bite. One involved someone who bit into baloney. This was my first that involved human flesh.

24/7: How do bitemarks compare to fingerprints?

DR. SOUVIRON: Bitemarks are not anywhere near as accurate as fingerprints. Fingerprints never change. Your print when you're ten years old is the same print as when you're 50 years old. But teeth can change. You can cap teeth, pull teeth. You can put braces on and change teeth.

24/7: What makes one bite easier to identify than another bite?

DR. SOUVIRON: The number of teeth that press down on the skin. More teeth makes it easier to identify a bite.

24/7: Do you study bitemarks differently today than you did in the 1970s?

DR. SOUVIRON: We follow a lot of the same steps. But we now use computers. We can scan teeth molds and bitemark photographs into the computer.

FORENSIC DOWNLOAD

Here's even more amazing stuff about forensic dentistry for you to chew on.

IN THIS SECTION:

- how CHEESE sent a man to jail;
- how FORENSIC DENTISTRY has been in the news;
- the TOOLS that are used to examine victims' teeth;
- whether forensic dentistry might be in YOUR FUTURE!

Key Dates in Forensic

1776 A Famous Patriot—and Dentist?

You've probably heard of Paul Revere. He was a hero of the American Revolution.

But did you know he was also a forensic dentist?

One of his patients was a man named Dr. Joseph Warren. Warren had a bad tooth. Revere made a bridge to replace it.

Not long after, Warren was killed in a big battle. He was buried with another soldier.

Months later, Revere was asked to identify Warren's body. The bodies had decayed. So Revere had to check their mouths. He found a body with the dental work he had done for Warren.

1978 Plane Crash Victims ID'd

After a terrible double plane crash in San Diego, California, a team of forensic dentists identified nearly 150 victims. It was the first time a non-military team used a computer program to match postmortem and antemortem records.

See Case #2: The Case of the Double Plane Crash.

1850 False Teeth Deliver Guilty Verdict

Dr. John Webster was on trial for the murder of Dr. George Parkman. The evidence? Some human remains—including some false teeth—had been found near Webster's lab.

Webster said the remains were from a corpse. But Parkman's dentist swore that the false teeth were Parkman's. The jury believed the dentist. It was the first time in U.S. history dental evidence put a murderer in jail!

1954 Cheese Chomper Goes to Jail

In Texas, a man robbed a grocery store and left a big clue behind. At the crime scene, police found a piece of cheese the robber had bitten into. Experts testified that the bitemark was probably the robber's. This was the first reported bitemark case in the U.S.

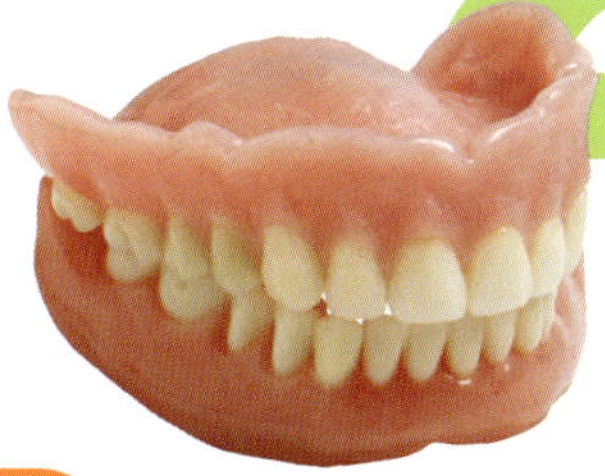

Dentistry

Who was the first person to ID victims by their teeth? Who first used bitemarks as evidence?

1979 Bitemark Evidence Conviction

Serial killer Ted Bundy was found guilty of murder, based on forensic bitemark evidence. The case "put **forensic odontology** on the map," says forensic dentist Tom David. This case proved that forensic dentists could do more than identify victims. They could help convict their killers.

See Case #3: The Case of the Strange Bite.

2005 The Forensic Dentist Club

Today, there are about 430 members in the odontology section of the American Academy of Forensic Sciences. When it became its own division in 1970, there were ten members.

In the News

Forensic dentistry is front-page news.

Dentists ID Thousands of Tsunami Victims

ADELAIDE, AUSTRALIA—May 2005

Forensic dentists from Adelaide joined dentists from all over the world in Thailand. The dentists helped to identify victims of the tsunami that struck on December 26, 2004, in the Indian Ocean.

About 230,000 people died from the giant wave and the flooding that followed. "The bodies to be identified just kept on coming," said Dr. Helen James from the Australian team.

Now, five months later, the work is done. Experts say that 87 percent of the identifications were done by forensic dentists. Nine percent of the victims were identified by their fingerprints. Less than one percent were identified by DNA evidence.

In December 2004, a tsunami struck in the Indian Ocean. Here, it hits the shore in Thailand.

In August 2005, the city of New Orleans was flooded after Hurricane Katrina. Here, a car is pinned under a house.

Dental Records Used to ID Katrina Victims

U.S. GULF COAST—October 2005

In the wake of Hurricane Katrina, hundreds of victims have not been identified. Katrina struck on August 29, 2005, devastating much of the Gulf Coast. Rescue efforts were delayed.

By the time bodies were found, many were too damaged to identify. Louis Cataldie, the Louisiana medical examiner, explains that he is relying on forensic dentistry to identify these victims. "Dental records are a great solution," he said. "A good dental record is akin . . . to a good fingerprint."

An investigator on the scene after Hurricane Katrina.

Say Ahhh!

Have a look at the tools, equipment, charts, forms, and other stuff used by a forensic dentist.

UNIVERSAL NUMBERING SYSTEM

Say a forensic dentist is trying to ID a victim. She examines the victim's teeth. Then she compares them to antemortem records from other dentists' offices. The records have information about patients' teeth. But how does the forensic dentist know which teeth the information refers to?

Dentists use the Universal Numbering System. In this system, each tooth has a number. Have a look.

The patient's upper back tooth on the right side is tooth #1. The numbers then go around the top. Tooth #17 is the lower back tooth on the left side.

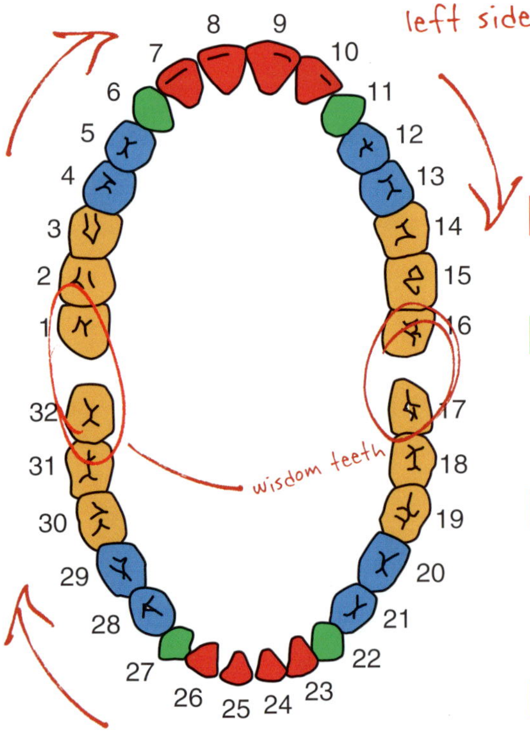

TYPES OF TEETH

As you can see, you have four kinds of teeth.

incisors Those are eight teeth in the front of the mouth. They're used to cut food.

canines They're also called **cuspids**. They're the four sharp, pointy ones toward the front of your mouth.

premolars They're also called **bicuspids**. They're the eight teeth with two points toward the back of your mouth. They're used to tear and grind food.

molars Those are the 12 teeth in the back of the mouth that grind food.

VICTIM ID CHARTS

When forensic dentists are trying to identify victims, they use these forms. Notice how each tooth is referred to by its number from the Universal Numbering System.

On the postmortem form, the dentist records information about the victim's teeth.

On the antemortem form, the dentist takes notes about the victim's old dental records.

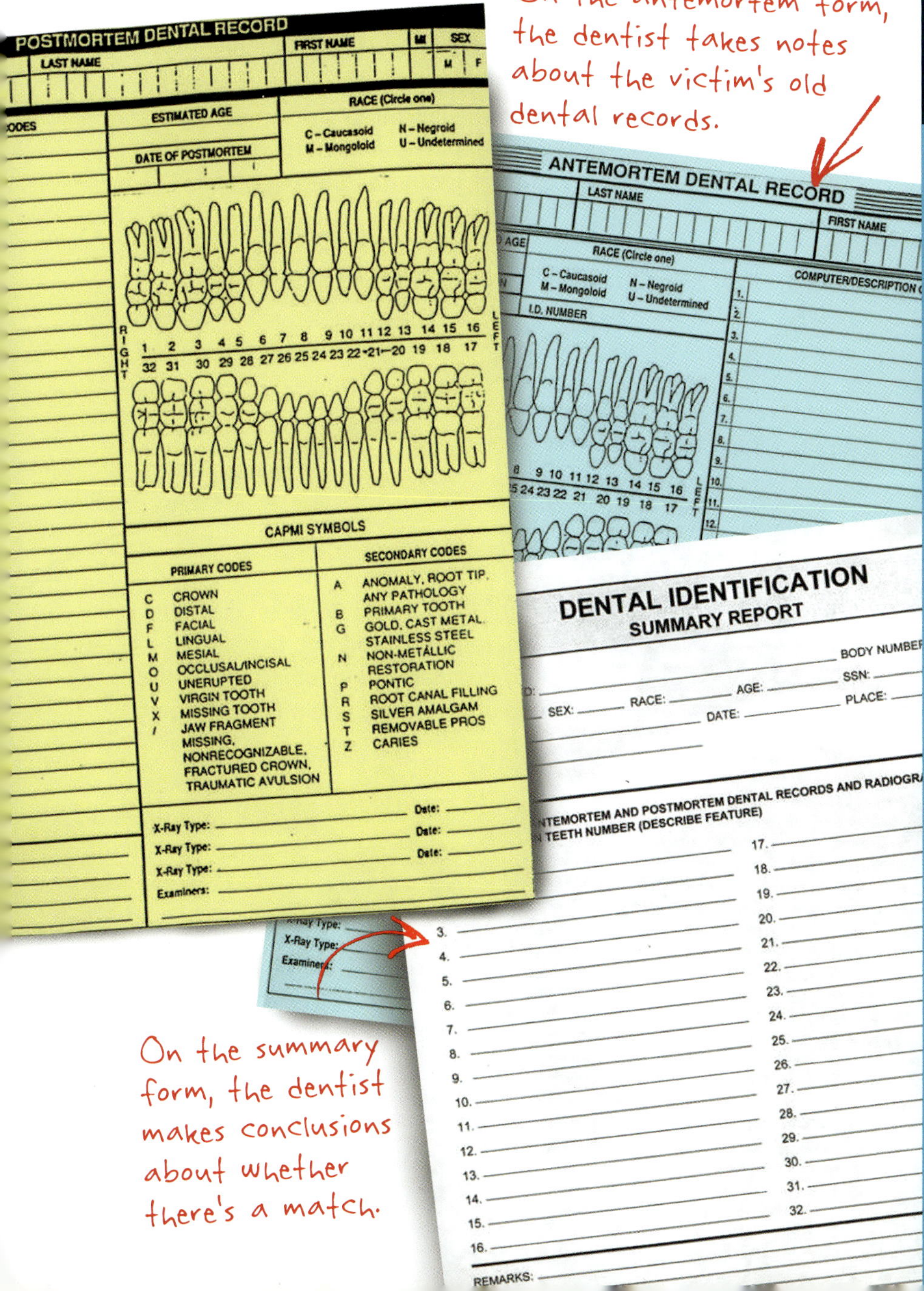

On the summary form, the dentist makes conclusions about whether there's a match.

TOOLS AND EQUIPMENT

TOOLS

dental mirror Think of this as a mirror on a stick. This tool allows a forensic dentist to get a good look at all the teeth—even the teeth in the back of the mouth. Perhaps she'll want to see if the victim still has **wisdom teeth**. Are the molars in good shape? How many fillings does the victim have? Are any teeth fractured or broken?

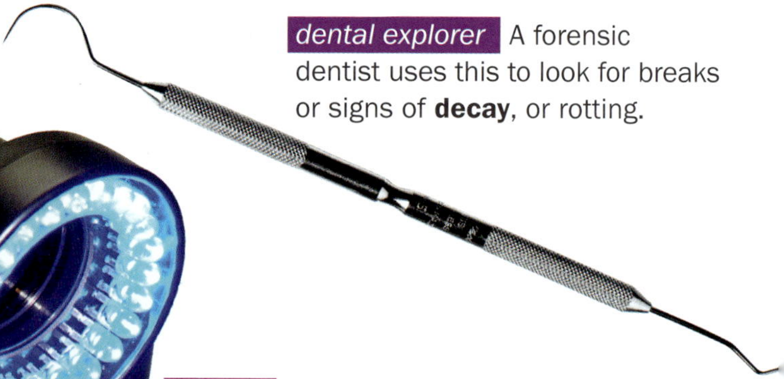

dental explorer A forensic dentist uses this to look for breaks or signs of **decay**, or rotting.

camera Forensic dentists use special cameras to photograph bitemarks. They compare the photographs to the model they make of a suspect's teeth.

x-rays An x-ray is a stream of radiation used to take a picture. X-rays allow dentists to look inside a tooth. Forensic dentist often x-ray victims' teeth. Then they compare these postmortem x-rays to antemortem x-rays.

[Forensic Fact]
Dentists and physicians call their tools "instruments."

alginate Forensic dentists mix this material with water. The mixture is similar to a sticky Play-Doh. In bitemark cases, forensic dentists use this mixture to make a copy of a suspect's teeth.

digital imaging In the early 1990s, forensic dentists began using this new technology for taking x-rays. With digital imaging, an image of the teeth shows up on the computer screen. A dentist can look at these images instantly.

WinID Computer Program

How It Works: First, dental records are entered into the program. Then, the program searches the database. It compares antemortem against postmortem records. It then comes up with a list of the most likely matches.
How It Has Improved: The program was written in 1988. After 9/11/01, the WinID program was rewritten. Now dentists can input written dental records and graphic data, such as x-rays.

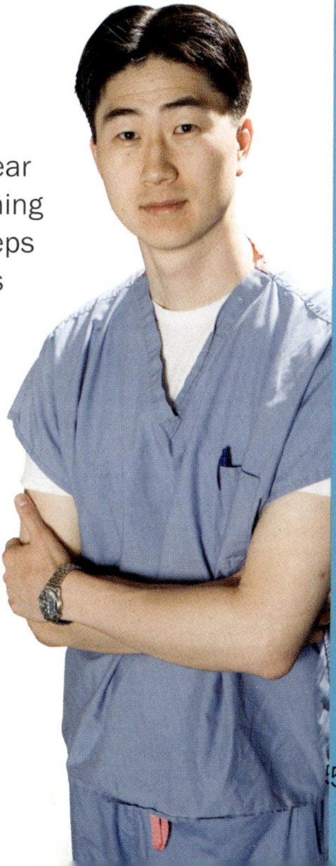

CLOTHING

face mask Forensic dentists wear masks to keep them from breathing dangerous chemicals. It also keeps them from breathing in germs as dead bodies begin to rot.

scrubs Forensic dentists wear scrubs when they do postmortem examinations. By doing this, they don't get harmful stuff on their clothes.

aprons and gloves Forensic dentists do some dirty work. Aprons and gloves protect them from blood and other goo.

HELP WANTED:

Forensic Dentist

Is forensic dentistry something that you could sink your teeth into? Here's more information about this field.

Dr. Skip Sperber is a forensic dentist in CA.

Q&A: DR. SKIP SPERBER

24/7: You're now a well-known forensic dentist. What was your first job in the field?

DR. SPERBER: [Before college, I worked in the toxicology department of the medical examiner's office in New York City.] My responsibilities included going up to the **autopsy** room. That's where dead bodies are examined. I'd collect tissue samples from the bodies. Then I'd bring these samples to toxicologists. They tested the tissues for chemicals and poisons.

24/7: How did you end up practicing forensic dentistry in San Diego, California?

DR. SPERBER: My father was a dentist. He had an office in New York City. He had famous patients like Babe Ruth, the great baseball hero. After college, I decided to follow in his footsteps and go to dental school. [Later,] I started a private practice in San Diego. One of my patients introduced me to San Diego County's coroner. The coroner needed a forensic dentist. He wanted someone who wasn't afraid to look at dead, mangled bodies.

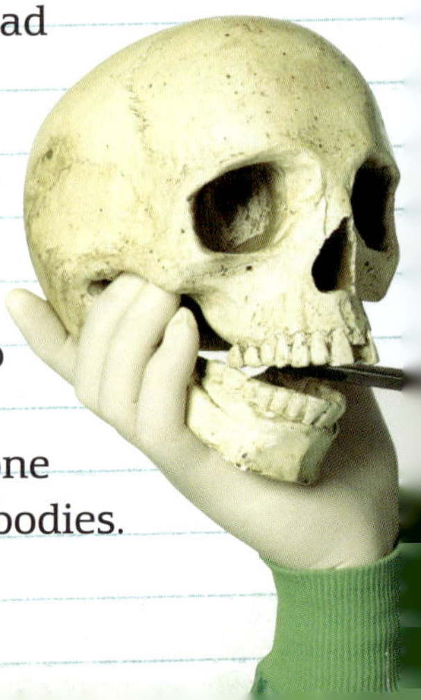

24/7: You were part of a team that helped identify victims of the terrorist attacks on September 11, 2001. What was the most upsetting thing about the experience?

DR. SPERBER: I was just struck by all the photographs that had been posted all over the streets by family and friends of the victims. It was incredibly sad because I realized that many of the people in the buildings weren't going to come back to their families or loved ones.

THE STATS

DAY JOB: Most forensic dentists spend most of their time as regular dentists.

MONEY: The average yearly salary for a dentist in the U.S. is about $194,000. When they work on cases, forensic dentists are often paid $300 an hour or even more.

EDUCATION: Forensic dentists must finish:

- 4 years of college;
- 4 years of dental school;
- forensic dentistry training courses.

THE NUMBERS: There are about 430 forensic dentists in the American Academy of Forensic Sciences.

24/7: Are there challenges facing forensic dentistry today?

DR. SPERBER: People have fewer cavities today than they did 50 years ago. That's because of the use of **fluorides**. So we find fewer and fewer unique features, like crowns or fillings or bridges, when we examine victims' teeth. We have to develop a computer program that allows us to input the shape of a tooth or root so we can identify victims who haven't had much dental work done.

DO YOU HAVE WHAT IT TAKES?

Take this totally unscientific quiz to find out if forensic dentistry might be a good career for you

1. **How are you at solving problems?**
   a) I'm great at finding solutions.
   b) Sometimes I have good ideas.
   c) You'd better ask someone else.

2. **Are you interested in how the body works?**
   a) I read everything I can find about the human body.
   b) I think it's sort of interesting.
   c) I'm only interested in my next meal.

3. **Are you good in an emergency?**
   a) I can always stay calm.
   b) I can usually keep my head.
   c) I jump at any noise.

4. **Do you get grossed out?**
   a) In fact, I like to watch operations on TV.
   b) I don't mind the sight of blood.
   c) I feel sick just thinking about that question.

5. **Are you interested in solving crimes?**
   a) Yes. I want criminals put in jail.
   b) I like to watch crime shows on TV.
   c) Someone else can do that.

YOUR SCORE

Give yourself 3 points for every "**a**" you chose. Give yourself 2 points for every "**b**" you chose. Give yourself 1 point for every "**c**" you chose.

If you got **13–15 points**, you'd probably be a good forensic dentist.
If you got **10–12 points**, you might be a good forensic dentist.
If you got **5–9 points**, you might want to look at another career!

HOW TO GET STARTED . . . NOW!

It's never too early to start working toward your goals.

GET AN EDUCATION

- Starting now, take classes in biology, chemistry, physics, health, and math.
- Start thinking about college. Look for ones that have good pre-dental programs.
- Read the newspaper. Keep up with what's going on in your community.
- Read anything you can find about forensic dentistry.
- See the books and Web sites in the Resources section on pages 56-58.
- Graduate from high school!

NETWORK!

- Ask your own dentist for advice about becoming a dentist.
- Find out about forensic groups in your area.

GET AN INTERNSHIP

- Look for an internship with a dentist.
- Look for an internship in a forensics lab.

LEARN ABOUT OTHER JOBS IN THE FIELD

- **Dental hygienists.** They help with postmortem exams and collecting antemortem dental records. They take x-rays and clean and examine teeth. Education? The training program usually takes about two years. Average salary is $50,000.
- **Dental assistants.** They may also help out with postmortem exams and collecting records. Education? A high school diploma. Also, they must graduate from a training program. That program usually takes between nine and 11 months. Average salary is $28,000.

Resources

Looking for more information about forensic dentistry? Here are some resources you don't want to miss!

PROFESSIONAL ORGANIZATIONS

American Academy of Forensic Sciences (AAFS)

www.aafs.org
410 North 21st Street
Colorado Springs, CO 80904-2798
PHONE: 719-636-1100
FAX: 719-636-1993

The AAFS provides education for people interested in working in forensics and continuing education for experts already in the field. The organization runs workshops and sessions at its annual meeting that are open to students in middle school and up.

American Board of Forensic Odontology (ABFO)

www.abfo.org
E-MAIL: webmaster1@abfo.org

The ABFO sets guidelines for practicing forensic dentistry. It also grants certification for forensic dentists who have the necessary experience and training and also pass a tough exam.

American Dental Association (ADA)

www.ada.org
211 East Chicago Ave.
Chicago, IL 60611-2678
PHONE: 312-440-2500

With more than 153,000 members, the ADA is the nation's largest dental association. It occasionally offers workshops for dental professionals who wish to learn more about forensic dentistry.

American Society of Forensic Odontology (ASFO)

www.forensicdentistryonline.org
Non-members can buy the ASFO's *Manual of Forensic Odontology* online for $79.
MAILING ADDRESS:
P.O. Box 1989
Eureka, MT 55917-0989
FAX: 001-250-426-7282
E-MAIL: docgib@cyberlink.bc.ca

The ASFO has more than 1,000 members in 26 countries. The group is open to anyone interested in forensic dentistry.

Bureau of Legal Dentistry (BOLD Lab)

www.boldlab.org
6190 Agronomy Road
Suite 202
Vancouver, British Columbia
Canada V6T 1Z3
PHONE: 604-822-8822
E-MAIL: boldlab@interchange.ubc.ca

BOLD Lab is North America's first and only laboratory devoted full-time to research, casework, and graduate teaching in forensic dentistry. The school offers a post-graduate degree.

Canadian Society of Forensic Science (CSFS)

www.csfs.ca
P.O. Box 37040
3332 McCarthy Road
Ottawa, Ontario
Canada K1V 0W0
PHONE: 613-738-0001
E-MAIL: csfs@bellnet.ca

The CSFS is open to professionals interested in forensic sciences. The group sends journals to its members four times a year. It also holds meetings, which include forensic workshops.

PROFESSIONAL TRAINING

Armed Forces Institute of Pathology (AFIP)

www.afip.org
6825 16th Street NW
Washington, DC 20306-6000
PHONE: 202-782-2100
EMAIL: owner@afip.osd.mil

The AFIP offers week-long courses in forensic dentistry for dental professionals.

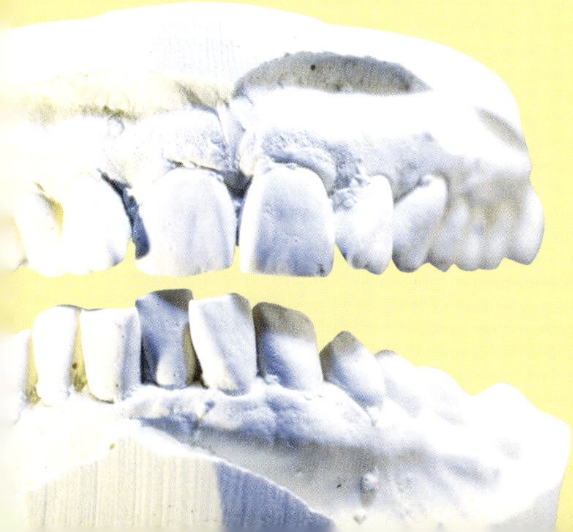

Disaster Mortuary Operational Response Team (DMORT)

www.dmort.org

DMORT teams are made up of volunteer forensic dentists and other types of forensic scientists. Teams respond after disasters when local officials ask for help.

University of Texas Health Science Center at San Antonio (UTHSCSA)

http://cde.uthscsa.edu/
7703 Floyd Curl Drive
San Antonio, TX 78229
PHONE: 210-567-3177
EMAIL: smile@uthscsa.edu

The Office of Continuing Dental Education offers workshops every other year for dental professionals—dentists, dental hygienists, and dental assistants—who are already practicing forensic dentistry or who wish to learn more.

PROFESSIONAL BOOKS

Bowers, Michael C. *Forensic Dental Evidence.* San Diego: Elsevier Academic Press, 2004.

Stimson, Paul G., and Curtis A. Mertz, eds. *Forensic Dentistry.* Boca Raton, FL: CRC Press, 1997.

BOOKS FOR KIDS ABOUT FORENSIC SCIENCE

Innes, Brian. *The Search for Forensic Evidence.* Milwaukee: Gareth Stevens, 2005.

Jones, Charlotte. *Fingerprints and Talking Bones: How Real-Life Crimes Are Solved.* New York: Yearling, 1999.

Lane, Brian. *Eyewitness: Crime & Detection.* New York: Dorling Kindersley, 1998.

Platt, Richard. *Forensics.* Boston: Kingfisher, 2005.

Silverstein, Herma. *Threads of Evidence: Using Forensic Science to Solve Crimes.* New York: 21st Century, 1997.

Walker, Pam, and Elaine Wood. *Crime Scene Investigations: Real-Life Science Labs for Grades 6–12.* San Francisco: Jossey-Bass, 1998.

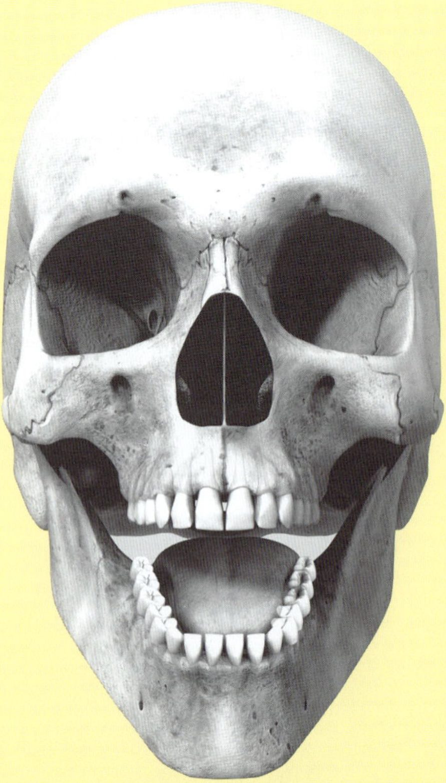

DENTAL MUSEUM

National Museum of Dentistry
www.dentalmuseum.umaryland.edu
31 South Greene Street
Baltimore, MD 21201-1504
PHONE: 410-706-0600
FAX: 410-706-8313

Dictionary

A

antemortem (an-tee-MORE-tehm) *adjective* before death

autopsy (AW-top-see) *noun* examination of a body after death

B

bicuspid (bye-KUSS-pid) *noun* a tooth with two points that tear and grind food. Bicuspids are also called *premolars*.

bitemark (BYTE-mark) *noun* a mark from someone's teeth left on skin or other surfaces

bridge (brij) *noun* a thing glued in the mouth to replace missing teeth

C

canines (KAY-nines) *noun* the sharp teeth in the front of your mouth. They're also called *cuspids*.

coroner (CORE-un-er) *noun* someone hired by the government to investigate sudden and mysterious deaths

corpse (korps) *noun* a dead body

crown (crown) *noun* the part of the tooth that can be seen (above the gums). It's also something made to cover a damaged tooth. A crown can be made of porcelain, plastic, or metal. It helps bring back the function and look of a tooth.

cuspids (CUS-pids) *noun* same as canines

D

decay (dee-KAY) *noun* the rotten or broken-down part of a tooth

dental assistant (DIN-tuhl a-SIS-tant) *noun* someone who helps a dentist and/or a dental hygienist care for a patient. Dental assistants often do teeth cleanings and talk to a patient about proper dental care.

dental explorer (DIN-tuhl ex-PLORE-er) *noun* a tool with a sharp point that a dentist uses to find cracks or signs of decay

dental hygienist (DEN-tuhl hi-JEN-ist) *noun* someone who helps patients prevent dental problems. They often take x-rays and clean teeth.

dental mirror (DEN-tuhl MIHR-ore) *noun* a tool that a dentist uses to look at teeth and other features in the mouth

dental records (DEN-tuhl REK-urds) *noun* the notes and x-rays your dentist keeps about your teeth

dentist (DEN-tists) *noun* someone trained to care for the teeth, gums, and other tissues in the mouth

digital imaging (DIJ-ih-tull IM-uh-jing) *noun* a way of taking pictures of teeth and gums. The image taken of a person's mouth goes directly to the computer screen.

DNA (dee-en-ay) *noun* a chemical found in almost every cell of your body. No two people have the same DNA (except identical twins).

dupe (doop) *noun* a copy. It's short for the word *duplicate*.

E

enamel (ee-NA-mull) *noun* the hard, white stuff that covers most of each tooth

expert (EK-spurt) *noun* a person with special knowledge or experience. See page 12 for a list of forensic experts.

F

FBI (EF-bee-eye) *noun* a group in the U.S. government that investigates major crimes. It stands for *Federal Bureau of Investigation*.

filling (FIL-ing) *noun* stuff used to fill a tooth after the dentist has scraped out the decayed part

fluoride (FLOOR-ide) *noun* stuff that dentists put on teeth to make them stronger

forensic anthropologist (fore-EN-zick an-THRO-pol-oh-jist) *noun* someone who is called in to identify mysterious bones

forensic dentist (fore-EN-zick DEN-tist) *noun* someone who identifies victims and criminals by their teeth or bitemarks

forensic odontology (fore-EN-zick OH-don-TOL-oh-gee) *noun* a science that involves the handling, examination, and evaluation of dental evidence. It's also called *forensic dentistry*.

I

ID (eye-DEE) *verb* to find who a person is. It's short for *identify*.

identify (eye-DEN-tuh-fye) *verb* to find out who someone is

impacted (im-PAK-ted) *adjective* describing a tooth that can't grow out because it is stuck against another tooth or is under bone or soft tissue. Wisdom teeth are often impacted.

incisors (in-SIZE-ers) *noun* teeth located in front of the canines on the upper and lower jaws. These sharp-edged teeth cut food.

M

microscope (MYE-croh-skope) *noun* a tool used by scientist. A microscope makes objects look bigger.

molars (mole-ERS) *noun* teeth near the back of the upper and lower jaws, behind the incisors and canines. These teeth have wide crowns that grind food.

O

odontology (OH-don-TOL-oh-gee) *noun* dentistry; the study of teeth

P

postmortem (pohst-MORE-tehm) *adjective* after death

premolars (pre-MOLE-ers) *noun* teeth between the canines (cuspids) and the molars on the upper and lower jaws. These teeth have two points that tear and grind food. They are also called *bicuspids*.

R

reefer (REE-fur) *noun* a large refrigerated trailer used to store bodies

root (rute) *noun* the part of a tooth that attaches it to the bone

S

serial (SEER-ee-uhl) *adjective* performing similar acts or crimes over time

T

trace (trayss) *noun* evidence of something

V

victim (VICK-tim) *noun* a person who is harmed or killed

W

wisdom teeth (WIZ-dum teeth) *noun* the last teeth (or eighth tooth from the middle) on the upper and lower jaws.

X

x-ray (ex-RAY) *noun* a stream of radiation used to take a picture

Index

Photo Credits: Alamy Images: 4 left, 8 (Comstock Images), 10 (David Hoffman Photo Library), cover (Garry Gay), 35 (Andre Jenny), 4 right, 11 (Dieter Melhorn), 10 (Peter Arnold, Inc.), 55 (Stockdisc Classic), 10 (Maximilian Weinzeirl), 52 bottom, 53 (WoodyStock); Ann Norrlander: 20; AP/Wide World Photos: 24 (courtesy KARE-TV), 19 top (Charles Curtis/ Duluth News-Tribune), 40 (Mark Levy), 5 top, 18, 19 bottom (Jim Mone), 21 bottom (Angie Riebe), 33 (Dan Trevan), 5 bottom, 41 bottom; Corbis Images: 5 center, 28, 36, 38 (Bettmann), 11, 14 left, 22 (Kul Bhatia/zefa), 44 top (Geoffrey Clements), 25 (George B. Diebold), 15 (Raymond Gehman), 46 (Jeremy Horner), 10, 27, 50 bottom, 57 (Royalty-Free), 29, 44 bottom (Vince Streano), 32 (Julian Abram Wainwright/epa); David Lindroth: 17, 26, 37; Dr. Norman Sperber/Photo Express: 34, 52 top; Courtesy of Dr. Richard Souviron: 39, 41 top; ForensicDentalServices/www.forensicdentistryonline.org: 49; Getty Images: 58 (3D4Medicalcom), 47 top (Robyn Beck/AFP), 6 top, 45 bottom (C Squared Studios), 51 top left (George Doyle & Ciaran Griffin/Stockdisc Classic), back cover, 6 bottom, 50 top and center right (Gary Faye), 45 top (FoodCollection), 47 bottom (Chris Graythen), 51 right (K. Hatt/Photodisc Green), 10 (Jonathan Kim/Photographer's Choice), 10 (Mario Lalich/Riser), 21 top (Spike Mafford/Photodisc Green), 3 (Guillaume Simoneau/fStop), 10 (Donn Thompson/DK Stock); Ian Hunter/ www.policensw.com: 2 center and bottom; James Levin Studios: 1 center, 2 top, 23, 51 bottom left; Miami-Dade County Medical Examiner Department, Forensic Imaging Bureau: 42; Robertstock.com/BrandX: 10, 30; Sirchie Fingerprint Laboratories: 1 left, 54; St. Paul Pioneer Press/Craig Borck: 16; The Lee Harvey Oswald Research Page/The Norton Report: 14 top right; VEER/Miguel Angel Munoz/age fotostock: 10; www.clouddome.com: 50 center left

Author's Note

THE PROS KNOW: In my research for this book, I found it most helpful to talk and e-mail with experts. I had countless phone conversations and e-mail exchanges with Dr. Tom David, Dr. Ann Norrlander, and Dr. Skip Sperber in particular. But how do you find an expert who's willing to talk?

Start with your dentist. Maybe he or she has worked on forensic dental cases and can talk to you about the experience. Or maybe your dentist has a friend who does forensic dentistry work.

I started my research by contacting Dr. Sperber because I have a connection to him. He put me in touch with Dr. Norrlander. How does he know her? You might recall that at the trial for the murder of Katie Poirier, another forensic dentist testified. This expert did not agree that the tooth likely belonged to Katie. That forensic dentist was Dr. Sperber!

If your dentist can't help, contact the American Academy of Forensic Sciences (AAFS). I did. About 430 forensic dentists belong to the odontology section of the AAFS. The group might be willing to give you an e-mail address for one of its members. That is how I began to e-mail with Dr. David, and he was a huge help to me. He reviewed sections of the book to make sure what I wrote was correct. He also explained things that I didn't understand.

SEE FOR YOURSELF: If you find a forensic dentist in your area, be bold and ask if you could shadow him or her on the job for a day. The worst that the dentist can say is no. And if that happens, don't worry. I have another idea ...

The AAFS offers workshops and sessions each year when it meets and they are open to students in middle school and up. This is a wonderful opportunity to learn more about the field from experts.

Finally, be open to any opportunity you have to learn about forensics. Dr. Sperber's first experience with forensics was working in a toxicology lab. Today he is considered one of the country's top forensic dentists. Look what that experience helped him to achieve!

ACKNOWLEDGMENTS

I would like to thank the following forensic dentists for taking the time to talk about their work. Without their help, this book would not be possible: Dr. Jeffrey Burkes, Dr. Tom David, Dr. Lowell Levine, Dr. Ann Norrlander, Dr. Richard Souviron, and Dr. Skip Sperber. Thank you also to Kenneth Field and Kimberly Wrasse at the American Academy of Forensic Sciences.

CONTENT ADVISER: Dr. L. Thomas Johnson, Professor, Dental Science, Forensic Dentistry & Public Health, Marquette University